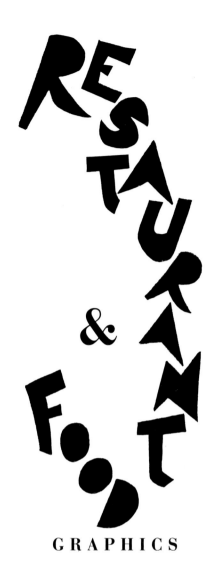

RESTAURANT & FOOD

GRAPHICS

Judi Radice Hays

with the
NATIONAL
RESTAURANT
ASSOCIATION

Graphic Details
An Imprint of PBC International, Inc.

Distributor to the book trade in the United States and Canada

Rizzoli International Publications Inc.

300 Park Avenue South

New York, NY 10010

Distributor to the art trade in the United States and Canada

PBC International, Inc.

One School Street

Glen Cove, NY 11542

Distributor throughout the rest of the world

Hearst Books International

1350 Avenue of the Americas

New York, NY 10019

Library of Congress Cataloging–in–Publication Data

Hays, Judi Radice
    Restaurant & food graphics / by Judi Radice Hays with the
National Restaurant Association
    p. cm.
    Includes indexes.
    ISBN 0–86636–287–8   (0-86636-376-9 pbk)
    1. Menu design—United States   I. National Restaurant
    Association (U.S.) II. Title III. Restaurant & food graphics
NC1002.M4R35 1994   93–49501
741.6—dc20   CIP

CAVEAT– Information in this text is believed accurate, and will pose no problem for the
student or casual reader. However, the author was often constrained by information
contained in signed release forms, information that could have been in error or not
included at all. Any misinformation (or lack of information) is the result of failure in
these attestations. The author has done whatever is possible to insure accuracy.

Photography by Naum Kazhdan, 58 Third Street, Brooklyn, New York, 11218
unless otherwise noted.

Separation by Fine Arts Repro House Co., LTD., Hong Kong

Printing and Binding by C&C Joint Printing Co., (H.K.) LTD., Hong Kong

Printed in Hong Kong

10 9 8 7 6 5 4 3 2 1

To my true companion,
Eddy Hays

TABLE OF CONTENTS

 Denotes the National Restaurant Association's Great Menu Contest winners.

FOREWORD

There's a well-worn cliché in the restaurant business about customers "eating" with their eyes before a fork ever touches the plate. That is a shorthand way of saying that using care to present food in an attractive way is just as important as the attention paid to selecting and preparing it.

But before the customer ever sees the food, there is the menu—the centerpiece of the restaurant's graphic identity system.

Without question, the menu is the best marketing tool a restaurateur can have. It can entice customers, it can educate them, it can amuse, and it can confuse. But more than anything else, it is a reflection of a restaurant's reason for being. If it is possible to capture a restaurant's soul on paper, then a menu does just that. Good or bad, like it or not, a menu will tell a customer what to expect. What do I mean? Some examples:

- oversized menu printed on heavy stock, type in flowing script tells me I'm due to get a thank you note from my credit card company.

- sharp, snappy descriptions on quality recycled stock says young and energetic minds and hands in the kitchen.

- text that leaves no room for interpretation, describes each item so thoroughly a customer could use it as a recipe, tells me the chef is fussy, uptight and meticulous...so is the food.

- a laser-printed insert with today's date on it hints what's on my plate will be fresh and peak of season.

- plastic-coated menus with photographs of plated food prepare me for food that splatters and that rarely looks anything like the pictures.

- brand names on the menu—be they nationally advertised products or locally produced (I'm talking about mentions of Oreo cookie desserts, Smith and Jones Ice Cream, and statements like, "We only cook with Sinatra Olive Oil") tell me the kitchen cares enough to spend a little more for consistent quality.

It's simple. *Exciting* menu, *exciting* food. *Dull* menu, *dull* food.

For these and other factors, making menus exciting is becoming more interesting these days. For some, it feels like a revolution.

The widespread use of personal computers in restaurants of all sizes representing all market segments is a boon to restaurateurs and chefs who love to update their offerings and prices, fiddle with descriptions, experiment, or all of the above.

The genre has come a long way since the days of typed inserts. Easy-to-use graphic software and thousands of typefaces and clip-art choices make amateur menu designs accessible to the masses. Sure, most won't win any awards, but they do provide the flexibility to change something quickly and inexpensively.

Environmentally, the raising of consciousness about things Earth-friendly has cast another shadow over status-quo menu design. Restaurateurs are slowly coming to grips with the fact that their customers do care about such matters as recycling, re-use, composting, and air quality. Menus with a message, those that demonstrate a restaurateur's synergy with this movement, can get their philosophy across subtly (using menu paper stock that carries the recycled symbol) or overtly (a "mission statement" that spells out exactly what the restaurant is doing to manage its refuse).

Concerns about quality of recycled paper stock are dwindling for a couple of reasons. First, quality is very good today, though still somewhat pricy. Second, as more restaurants make at least some use of personal computers and their own laser printers, the question becomes almost moot.

I have said it often: If you want to know which way the restaurant industry goes, forget elaborate research—examine its menus. This book probes deeper than ever before into the journey to find the soul of America's restaurants. Enjoy the ride.

Michael DeLuca
Editor, *Restaurant Hospitality*

INTRODUCTION

The atmosphere in a restaurant is based on a variety of factors: the serving staff, their uniforms, the interior architecture, ambiance, lighting, color palette, food offerings and graphic design. All these elements play a part in the overall statement. If properly orchestrated, each of these elements will fit together into a seamless whole, helping to create a memorable experience for the customer.

The designer's challenge is to make the most of the graphic identity elements, using them to enhance and complement the themes apparent in the decor. Planned properly, a well-designed restaurant graphics program can be a powerful merchandising and promotional tool for the restaurant.

Designers have shown great imagination in making many of the restaurant graphics an extension of the restaurants' personalities. Colors are drawn from the decor, and in some instances, certain architectural elements or materials are used to reinforce them. The result of the interaction between designer and restaurateur reveals better communication than ever before.

Menus, matches, T-shirts, posters, exterior signage and other graphic expressions have become a new frontier in establishing restaurants' identities because they are just as much a promotional vehicle for the restaurant as they are an art form. As the pieces in this book demonstrate, there are virtually no limits on what can be achieved, both aesthetically and in a marketing sense. The surge of interest in food, and the greater awareness of design have resulted in an increase in the number of entries in contests for excellence in menu design, such as The Great Menu Contest sponsored by the National Restaurant Association. Winners of this contest are designated in this book with a blue ribbon.

In this book, we have carefully selected the most innovative, well-planned and attractive restaurant identities that prove that great design can be a wise investment.

Judi Radice Hays
San Francisco, California

1

Family & Casual Dining

restaurant
Stars

location
Hingham, Massachusetts

design firm
Marie P. Flaherty Arts & Design

designer/illustrator
Marie Flaherty Henderson

copywriter
Edward Kane

year produced
1992

CONCEPT

The designer updated the restaurant to the nineties, but kept a healthy respect for the origins of the building itself by incorporating design principles from past decades.

The amount of menu items increased, and the challenge was to add the new items without interrupting the flow of the menu, leaving enough empty space for the eye to rest. The illustrations were elongated vertically and horizontally to use the remaining space effectively.

Some of the foremost changes include illustrations based on human forms rather than animal forms, though a few remain. Human figures reflect the hot bed of activity that is in and around the restaurant.

SPECIAL VISUAL EFFECTS

The plates were prepared with a combination of knock-outs and overprints. The main heads and art were knock-outs.

STARTERS

shrimp cocktail	1.50/each
homemade boneless chicken fingers	4.25
boneless buffalo fingers	4.50
chicken wings – dozen	4.25
buffalo wings – dozen	4.50
ultimate nachos	4.95
fried calamari – sweet & tender	3.95
steamers	seasonal
mussels marinara	4.95
tomato, basil, wine garlic & parmesan cheese	
mozzarella sticks	3.95
homemade onion rings	3.25
potato skins	3.95
bacon & cheese broccoli & cheese	
STARS' combo	4.95
mozzarella sticks, chicken wings, onion rings	

SOUPS

	cup	bowl
soup of the day	1.75	2.50
onion soup au gratin	1.75	2.75
new england clam chowder	1.75	2.75

soup and ½ sandwich	
chicken salad	4.50
tuna salad	4.50
lobster salad	6.50

ASIDES

cottage cheese	1.25
cole slaw	1.25
vegetable	1.25
french fries	1.75
plain yogurt	1.00
fresh seasonal fruit	2.95

SALADS

house salad	2.25
chicken salad plate	5.25
garnished w/melon, grapes and walnuts	
tuna salad plate	5.25
garnished w/melon & grapes	
greek salad	4.25
served fresh w/toasted pita points	
chef salad	5.25
honey baked ham, swiss cheese, sliced turkey, tomatoes, onion, cucumbers, sprouts, & olives over a bed of lettuce	
spinach salad	4.95
w/hard boiled egg, mushrooms and bacon bits	
lobster salad	seasonal 8.95
garnished w/melon & grapes	
warm grilled chicken salad –	5.95
boneless breast grilled, sliced and served over a bed of mixed greens	
fresh fruit salad plate	4.95
fresh seasonal fruit w/yogurt or cottage cheese and banana bread	
ground sirloin plate	5.95
w/cottage cheese, lettuce, and tomato	

all salads and greens are served with fresh rolls, butter and your choice of dressing.

PIZZA

6" boboli pizza		with salad
cheese	3.50	4.75
pepperoni	3.95	5.25
sausage	3.95	5.25
pepper & onion	3.95	5.25
shrimp	4.50	5.75
canadian bacon	3.95	5.25
seasonal vegetable	3.95	5.25

additional toppings add 50¢, shrimp add $1.00

SANDWICHES

STARS clubs	
hamburger	4.75
cheeseburger	4.95
turkey	4.75
grilled reuben	4.95
hot pastrami	4.95
grilled boneless chicken	5.50
w/cheese	5.75
BBQ chicken special	5.95
grilled boneless chicken, topped with bacon, cheddar cheese, lettuce, tomato, and our own special bbq sauce. THE BEST!!	
chicken parmesan sandwich	5.50
cajun grilled chicken	5.50
w/cheese	5.75
grilled chicken	5.95
w/roasted red peppers and mozzarella cheese	
grilled swordfish sandwich	6.95
w/monterey jack cheese	
steak tips & cheese sandwich	4.95
fried fish sandwich	4.25
w/cheddar cheese	4.50
chicken salad sandwich	4.75
tuna salad sandwich	4.75
lobster salad sandwich – seasonal	7.95
fried clam roll	seasonal
BLT	3.95

HEARTY SANDWICHES

turkey	4.95
on whole grain bread w/muenster cheese, lettuce, tomato, sprouts, & served with honey mustard	
roast beef	4.95
on whole grain bread w/boursin cheese, lettuce, tomato & sprouts	
honey baked ham	4.95
on whole grain bread w/swiss cheese, lettuce, tomato, sprouts, & sweet honey mustard	
STARS vegetable	4.25
on whole grain bread w/muenster cheese, lettuce, tomato, sprouts, & sweet honey mustard & garnished w/melon & grapes instead of fries	

all sandwiches served with a pickle and fries on your choice of bulkie roll, onion roll, white, whole wheat, rye bread, or pita bread.

KABOBS

chicken	6.95
steak tips	6.95
shrimp	7.95

all marinated in a special sauce and skewered with red and yellow peppers and onions.

ENTREES

grilled swordfish	9.95
grilled cajun swordfish	9.95
grilled salmon	8.95
w/citrus butter	
broiled scrod	6.25
broiled scallops	7.95
fish & chips	5.95
fried clam plate	seasonal
fried scallops	6.95
fried calamari	5.95
fried shrimp	8.95
steak tips	6.50
bbq or teriyaki	
double thick pork chop	7.95
boneless chicken breast	6.50
bbq or teriyaki	
grilled chicken	6.50
w/warm bacon sauce & a stuffed tomato	
caesar chicken	6.50
tender chicken breast, marinated in caesar dressing, grilled & topped w/mozzarella cheese	
roasted 1/2 chicken	6.95
w/rosemary & lemon	

all of the above are served with your choice of vegetable, rice or fries

BURGERS & BEERS OVER THERE

WORLD CLASS BEER CLUB

You are cordially invited to attend the annual STARS and Tosca "Employee Christmas Gala"
Please join us for an evening of dining dancing celebration
semi-formal

Monday, December 13th, 1993

7 p.m. till 12:30 a.m.

The Chart House, Cohasset, Mass.

▲

Thank you for your help in making this past year a success.

STARS ★ Tosca

paper stock
Simpson Gainsborough Frost White

typefaces
Triset *(heads)*
Frutiger Condensed *(body copy)*

printing technique
Offset, Two-color Kamori Sprint

number of color inks
Three

number produced
400

design budget
$3,500

restaurant
Mustards Grill

location
Napa, California

design firm
Jim Moon Designs

designers
Michael Oulett
Jim Moon

illustrator
Jim Moon

copywriters
Bill Higgins
Michael Oulett
Jim Moon

year produced
1993

CONCEPT

Mustards' new menu perpetuates the same "country grill" feel as the original concept, complementing colors already inherent in the Mustards' logo. The menu was printed on a very durable and expensive stock. Mustards turns a lot of tables, so the durability issue was an important consideration.

General manager Michael Oulett wanted a fun, commemorative give-away for the restaurant's tenth anniversary, and came up with a 375mm wine bottle filled with mustard seed, which he had corked and foiled. Each customer received a bottle on the anniversary day.

Mustards' T-shirts lacked a spark that many tourists visiting the Napa Valley were looking for. The designer was asked to give the logo a new twist...something fun and eye-catching. He came up with the large brush stroke of the Mustards logo reversing through in red.

paper stock
Kimdura 12pt *(cover)*

typefaces
Calligraphy, American Typewriter

printing technique
Three PMS Colors with
U.V. Matte Book Lacquer

number of color inks
Three

number produced
2,500

design budget
$8,500

14

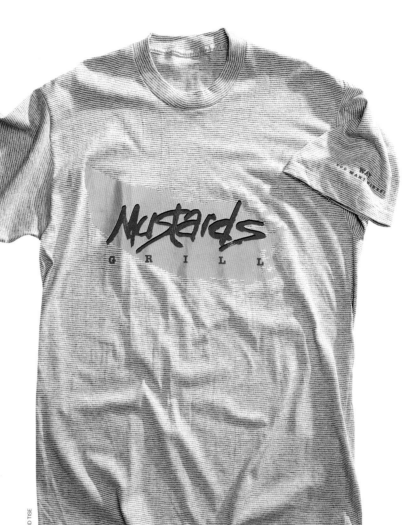

DAVID TISE

DAVID TISE

Appetizers, Soups and Salads

Different Soup every day	$ 3.50
Grilled Pasilla pepper, tamale stuffing, tomatillo salsa	5.95
Warm Goat Cheese with roasted beets and mixed greens	4.85
Grilled Asparagus with sherry vinaigrette and tarragon aioli crouton	6.50
Home Smoked Salmon with pasilla corn cakes and dill cream cheese	6.95
Grilled Chicken Skewer with peppers, shiitakes and miso dressing	5.75
Mixed Greens and Herbs, seasoned pecans, sherry vinaigrette	4.90
Caesar Salad	6.55
Oriental Chicken Salad	8.50
Thai Lamb and Ginger Salad, curry vinaigrette	7.95

From the Woodburning Grill and Oven.

Fresh Fish (see chalkboard)	A.Q.
Grilled Chicken Breast with roasted corn and tomatillo salsa (and spicy red beans)	10.95
Lemon and Garlic "mallet" Chicken with an array of summer vegetables	11.80
Smoked Long Island Duck with one hundred almond onion sauce	14.90
Grilled Rabbit with wild mushrooms and tarragon red wine sauce	15.95
Half slab Barbecued Baby Back Ribs with cornbread and slaw	10.95
Mongolian Pork Chop with braised sweet and sour cabbage	11.95
Calf's Liver with caramelized onions, bacon and homemade ketchup	9.90
Grilled Skirt Steak with thyme and garlic marinade	12.95
T Bone Lamb Chops with artichoke and onion ragout (and red onion relish)	17.95

We accept Cash, Mastercard, VISA, Diners Club & Carte Blanche.
Please, No American Express or Personal Checks.
Sales Tax will be added to everything Sold in the Bar and Dining Room.

Sandwiches

Hamburger or Cheeseburger	$ 6.95
Barbecued Chicken Breast with frenchfries and coleslaw	7.95
Grilled Ahi Tuna with basil mayonnaise and ginger	7.95
Salmon Club with remoulade	8.50

Sides and Condiments

Onion Rings	3.60
Roasted Garlic	2.75
Polenta with tomato and eggplant relish	2.95
Mashed Potatoes	1.95
Black Beans with chopped red onion, sour cream and chives	3.50
Homemade Ketchup	.75
Mustards Grill T-Shirt	12.00
Mustards Grill Sweatshirt	19.00

Desserts

Jack Daniel's Chocolate Cake with chocolate sauce	4.50
Lemon Meringue Pie with almond crust	4.25
Chocolate and Anise Brulee	3.95
Strawberry and Rhubarb Tart with vanilla cream	4.95
Crumble top Banana Cheesecake with caramel sauce	4.50
Caramel Hazelnut Apricot Tart with chocolate sauce and vanilla ice cream	4.75
Mocha Parfait with warm caramel sauce	4.50

restaurant
Tony's Town Square Restaurant

location
**Walt Disney World,
Lake Buena Vista, Florida**

design firm
Walt Disney World Design

designer
Mimi Palladino

illustrators
Peter Emslie *(Breakfast, Lunch/Dinner)*
Michael Mojher *(Lunch/Dinner)*
Jim Story *(Breakfast)*

year produced
1993

CONCEPT

For breakfast at Tony's, adults receive a copy of the *Main Street Gazette*, an authentic looking newspaper/menu that features a cover story about the restaurant, as well as other articles about the characters of the Disney film *Lady and the Tramp* and Main Street events. The newspaper/menu can be taken home as a souvenir.

Main Street, U.S.A. is an important part of the theme for the lunch menu. A depiction of Lady and the Tramp strolling along Main Street and a tip-on logo designed to evoke a feeling of old-world Italian are on the front cover. The inside cover is lined with a representation of the fabric used on the restaurant's chairs. A long illustration of Main Street is screened as a background for the menu copy to overprint. Each page reflects a frame of the illustration, as the characters from the film stroll down Main Street.

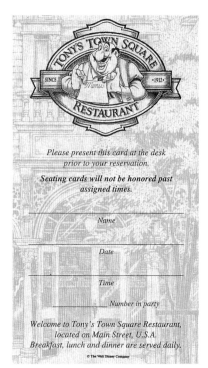

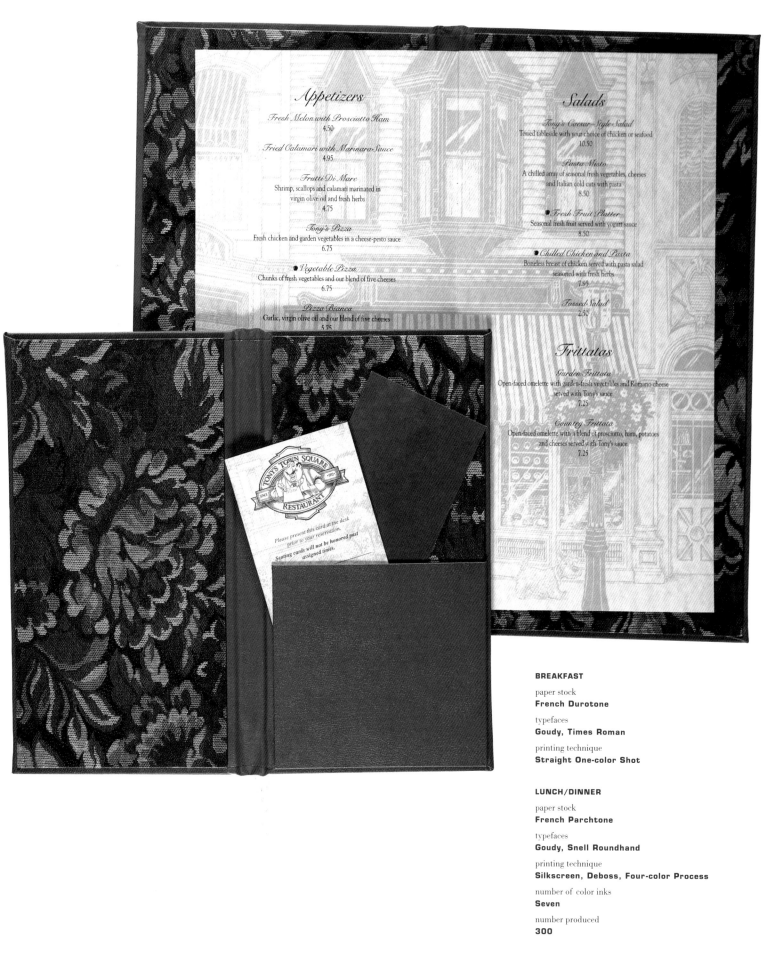

Appetizers

Fresh Melon with Prosciutto Ham
4.50

Fried Calamari with Marinara Sauce
4.95

Frutti Di Mare
Shrimp, scallops and calamari marinated in
virgin olive oil and fresh herbs
4.75

Tony's Pizza
Fresh chicken and garden vegetables in a cheese-pesto sauce
6.75

• *Vegetable Pizza*
Chunks of fresh vegetables and our blend of five cheeses
6.75

Pizza Bianca
Garlic, virgin olive oil and our blend of five cheeses
5.75

Salads

Tony's Caesar-Style Salad
Tossed tableside with your choice of chicken or seafood
10.50

Pasta Misto
A chilled array of seasonal fresh vegetables, cheeses
and Italian cold cuts with pasta
8.50

• *Fresh Fruit Platter*
Seasonal fresh fruit served with yogurt sauce
8.50

• *Chilled Chicken and Pasta*
Boneless breast of chicken served with pasta salad
seasoned with fresh herbs
7.95

Tossed Salad
2.50

Frittatas

Garden Frittata
Open-faced omelette with garden-fresh vegetables and Romano cheese
served with Tony's sauce
7.25

Country Frittata
Open-faced omelette with a blend of prosciutto, ham, potatoes
and cheeses served with Tony's sauce
7.25

BREAKFAST

paper stock
French Durotone

typefaces
Goudy, Times Roman

printing technique
Straight One-color Shot

LUNCH/DINNER

paper stock
French Parchtone

typefaces
Goudy, Snell Roundhand

printing technique
Silkscreen, Deboss, Four-color Process

number of color inks
Seven

number produced
300

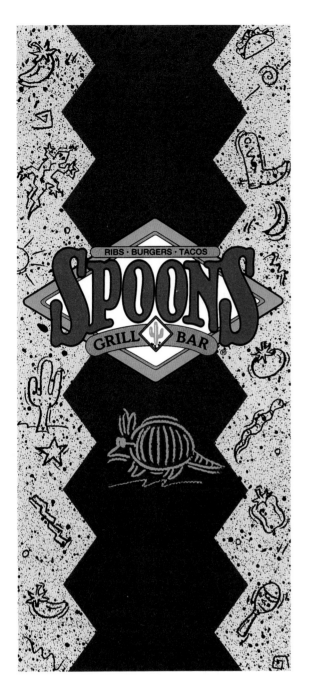

restaurant
Spoons Grill Bar

location
Newport Beach, California

design firm
Claude Prettyman Design

designer
Claude Prettyman

illustrators
Joy Pagaza
Claude Prettyman

copywriter
Michael Brawigan

year produced
1993

CONCEPT

Spoons' menu complements its personality through bright colors and both soft- and hard-edged graphics. The restaurant's interior motif is Tex-Mex, so those types of shapes, elements and colors add excitement and bring it all together.

TRENDS FOR THE '90s

"Menu formats and designs will vary greater with restaurant concepts, and menus will become more 'user-friendly.' "

paper stock
Simpson Sundance Felt White

typefaces
Cosmos, Willow

printing technique
Offset Lithography

number of color inks
Six

number produced
20,000

restaurant
Greenjeans

location
Calgary, Alberta, Canada

design firm
Guy Parsons Visual Communications Inc.

designer/illustrator
Guy Parsons

copywriter
John Reed

year produced
1993

CONCEPT

Adapting the painting *American Gothic* by Grant Wood, the menu reflects the fun and exciting atmosphere of this downtown restaurant and bar. By showing the characters letting their hair down and having fun, and staying with a simple relaxed color scheme with playful headings for the menu categories, the "fun" theme is reinforced.

TRENDS FOR THE '90s

"Obviously, the computer and its new tools and applications will have a huge influence in the appearance of menus. Less production time freed up by the computer will allow designers to spend more time on communication and the development of more effective designs."

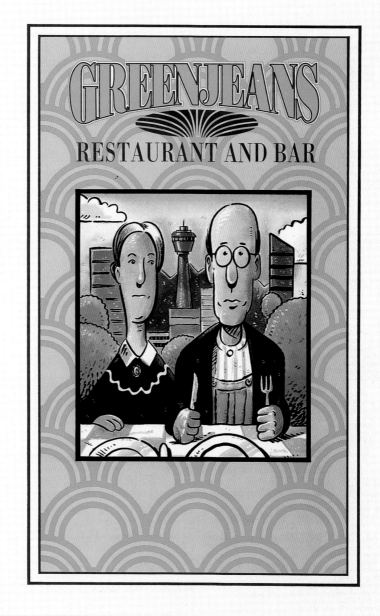

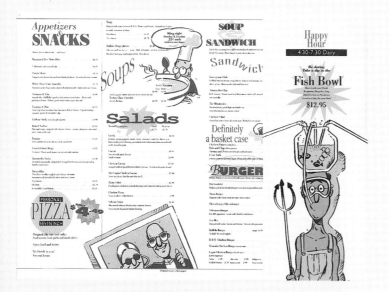

paper stock
Cornwall Dull *(cover)*

printing technique
Offset Lithography

number of color inks
Four-color Process

number produced
1,000

design budget
$500 *(design & illustration)*

19

restaurant
Coachmans Inn Restaurant

location
Edgerton, Wisconsin

design firm
Printing Image

designer/copywriter
Linda Begley–Korth

illustrator
Lisawn Porter

year produced
1993

CONCEPT

The Coachmans Inn's menus change daily
and are printed in-house. The menu covers
reflect the relaxed tourist and local hangout
atmosphere—both friendly and familiar.
The design also reflects the Inn's golf
course, resort and bar.

paper stock
Appleton

typeface
Goudy

number of color inks
Two

number produced
1,000

design budget
$1,200 *(including printing)*

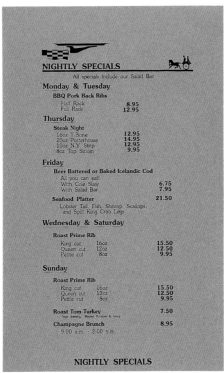

NIGHTLY SPECIALS
All specials include our Salad Bar

Monday & Tuesday

BBQ Pork Back Ribs
Half Rack		8.95
Full Rack		12.95

Thursday

Steak Night
16oz T-Bone		12.95
20oz Porterhouse		14.95
10oz N.Y. Strip		12.95
8oz Top Sirloin		9.95

Friday

Beer Battered or Baked Icelandic Cod
All you can eat!		
With Cole Slaw		6.75
With Salad Bar		7.95

Seafood Platter		21.50
Lobster Tail, Fish, Shrimp, Scallops, and Split King Crab Legs		

Wednesday & Saturday

Roast Prime Rib
King cut	16oz	15.50
Queen cut	12oz	12.50
Petite cut	8oz	9.95

Sunday

Roast Prime Rib
King cut	16oz	15.50
Queen cut	12oz	12.50
Petite cut	8oz	9.95

Roast Tom Turkey		7.50
Sage dressing, Mashed Potatoes & Gravy		
Champagne Brunch		8.95
9:00 a.m. - 2:00 p.m.		

NIGHTLY SPECIALS

Jeffrey Kadish

446 Columbus Avenue New York, NY 10024 ☎(212) 873-5025

restaurant
Main Street Restaurant

location
New York, New York

design firm
PM Design & Marketing

designer/illustrator
Philip Marzo

year produced
1993

CONCEPT

Main Street Restaurant serves traditional American food, family-style. Their menu's graphics have a simple, recognizable American feel, achieved through the combination of a classic American typeface and food icon (apple pie). A recycled paper stock and muted color palette convey an established, yet new look to the restaurant materials.

paper stock
Crosspointe Genesis

typefaces
Empire, Stone Sans

number of color inks
Two

number produced
500

design budget
Under $3,500

Dinner

Menu

American Family Style
All Dishes Serve 2-3

APPETIZERS

- Soup of the Day   *P/A*
- Iceburg Lettuce, Tomato and Blue Cheese Salad   *$11.00*
- Asparagus, White Cap Mushrooms and Georgia Pecan Salad   *$14.00*
- Grilled Gulf Shrimp Salad   *$16.00*
- Main Street Garden Salad with Sherry Vinaigrette   *$11.00*
- Grilled Vegetable and Cheese Pie   *$12.00*
- Crispy Vegetable Fritters   *$10.00*
- Corn Crusted Oysters with Tiger Sauce   *$16.00*
- Oven Roasted Chicken Wings with Orange Horseradish Marmalade   *$10.00*
- Kid's Fried Chicken Nuggets   *$10.00*
- Main Street Egg Rolls with Dipping Sauce   *$12.00*
- Walnut Sweet Potato Fries with Vermont Maple Dressing   *$6.50*
- Cajun Popcorn with Red Pepper Remoulade   *$15.00*

ENTREES

- Whole Roasted Fresh Herb Chicken   *$18.00*
- Deep Dish Chicken Pot Pie   *$18.00*
- Southern Fried Chicken   *$18.00*
- Roast Turkey Dinner with Fresh Cranberry Sauce and Stuffing   *$22.00*
- Manhattan Seafood Stew with Scallops, Shrimp, Oysters and Monkfish   *$32.00*
- Fresh Atlantic Salmon   *$26.00*
- Chesapeake Bay Crab Cakes with Dill Pickle Tartar Sauce   *$24.00*
- Grilled Fish of the Day   *P/A*
- Lime Marinated Seafood Salad with Mixed Greens   *$20.00*
- Rigatoni, Roasted Peppers, Tomato, Fennel and Mushrooms   *$16.00*
- Main Street's Macaroni and Cheese   *$10.00*
- Spaghetti with Chicken Meat Balls   *$15.00*
- Really Good Meatloaf   *$18.00*
- Grilled New York Sirloin   *$27.00*
- Big Earl's Blackened Pot Roast   *$22.00*
- Pork Chops and Apple Sauce   *$23.00*
- Uncle John's BBQ Beef Ribs   *$24.00*

SIDES - $6.50

- Mashed Potatoes (*All you can eat*)
- Blackened Mashed Potatoes
- Vegetable of the Day
- Main Street Apple Sauce
- Grilled Vegetable Platter
- Walnut Sweet Potato Fries
- Vegetable Casserole
- Spinach
- Grilled Corn on the Cob
- Grains, Rice, etc.

DESSERTS - $6.50

- Chocolate Pudding
- Fruit Pies
- Lemon Tart
- Brownie, Ice Cream and Chocolate Sauce
- Seasonal Fruit Crisp
- Chocolate Cake
- Peanut Butter Pie
- Ice Cream/Sundaes/Banana Split
- Jello (*24 Hour Notice Required*)

OPEN
seven nights a week

Ask to see our
weekend
Brunch menu

Please ask about our daily specials.

446 Columbus Avenue
New York, NY 10024

PHIL.LEO

restaurant
Houston's

location
Calgary, Alberta, Canada

design firm
Hoffman & Angelic Design

designer/calligrapher
Ivan Angelic

illustrator
Andrea Hoffman

year produced
1992

CONCEPT

Houston's interior decor brings to mind feelings of a stately country home with rustic flavor. Houston's "cowboy" image was changed to a more sophisticated "Western" image by focusing on the Western country (geographically) flavor that Houston's and the surrounding area naturally possess.

SPECIAL VISUAL EFFECTS

Each of the menus reflects a certain time of day, and the color theme reflects the seasons, as the menus will be used year-round. The children's menu is scaled down in size, but not in vibrancy and fun with its haystacks and cherry sun.

TRENDS FOR THE '90s

"Restaurants that care to have their menus designed want their restaurant, food and menu...to be of some entertainment value...at the same time cost cutting and environmental concerns have been creeping into our criteria. Consequently we as designers must be more clever and not rely on expensive tricks to wow the customer."

paper stock
Crosspointe Genesis

number of color inks
Five *(outside)* **Two** *(inside)*

restaurant
The Ground Round

location
Braintree, Massachusetts

design firm
The Baker Agency *(formerly Baker & Grooms)*

designers/illustrators
Jim Foster *(main)*
Mikie Baker *(place mats)*

photographer
David Bullock *(place mats)*

copywriter
Mikie Baker

year produced
1993

CONCEPT

The Ground Round's menu and related pieces have a playful illustrated look that identifies basic food items and gives a freshness message. Although the menu items and copy were revamped, and larger selections of beer and wine were added, the new menu design still works in the existing menu covers.

Related pieces include a table tent, coasters, a daily features card and "made for you with pride" card.

SPECIAL VISUAL EFFECTS

Playful graphics.

TRENDS FOR THE '90s

"Simple, easy to use menus that lead the customer through the ordering process. Use of new types of papers and more colorful graphics...."

paper stock
Champion Benefit Flax

typefaces
Bodoni, Stempel Schniedler

printing technique
Offset Lithography

number of color inks
Four

number produced
1,000

design budget
$25,000

restaurant
The Charcoal Grill Restaurant

location
Racine, Wisconsin

design firm
Printing Image

designer/copywriter
Linda Begley-Korth

illustrator
Lisawn Porter

year produced
1993

CONCEPT

The Charcoal Grill Restaurant's menu has a Southwestern feel and relays the restaurant's casual and comfortable environment. All of this was achieved within a limited budget.

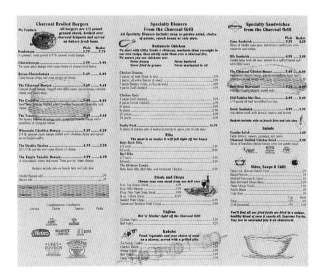

TRENDS FOR THE '90s

"Menu design should be more versatile and flexible. It should be easily adaptable to seasonal, weekly, and even daily changes."

paper stock
Concept *(Beckett-Butler Papers)*

typefaces
Piano, Delavan

printing technique
Offset Lithography

number of color inks
Two

number produced
50 breakfast *(laminated)*
50 dinner *(laminated)*
5,000 mini menus

design budget
$1,300

restaurant
Pork (Imagine the Possibilities)
(Holiday Inns)

location
Etobicoke, Ontario, Canada

design firm
Morris Graphics Ltd.

designers
John Zugec
Michael Moran

photographer
John Zugec

year produced
1993

CONCEPT

This menu was a joint project coordinated by Morris Graphics between the Ontario Pork Producers Marketing Board and Commonwealth Hospitality (a management company servicing 28 Holiday Inns in Canada). The content was developed by a Holiday Inn chef with input from Ontario Pork. The slogan was developed after reviewing the main content and understanding the menu's objective of adding fun and excitement for a six-week promotional period, extended because of its success.

Collateral materials include posters for the elevators, copies of the menus for the bedrooms, a special snack menu/bar card, and a content flyer/ballot. All items were produced in French and English.

TRENDS FOR THE '90s

"Product-specific menus and promotions are a great way to provide your customers with variety and keep them coming back to 'see what's new.' The most successful promotion items may also be considered as additions to your permanent menu."

paper stock
12pt Cornwall C2S

typefaces
Garamond, Linoscript, Lithos Bold

printing technique
Offset Lithography

number of color inks
Four-color Process

number produced
10,000

design budget
$20,000

restaurant
Tuft's

location
Ottawa, Ontario, Canada

design firm
Morris Graphics Ltd.

designers
Harvey Sedlack
Michael Moran

illustrator
Harvey Sedlack

copywriter
Michael Moran

year produced
1993

CONCEPT

Tuft's is a year-round restaurant operating in the stadium of the Ottawa Lynx RAA baseball team. Because the restaurant is a new franchise, the Tuft's menu is a give-away souvenir menu.

The cover depicts a locker with the restaurant's logo prominently displayed. Inside the "locker/menu," restaurant customers are treated to a light-hearted view of baseball. Effective graphics highlight key menu sections and/or items providing excellent menu merchandising. The back page sells souvenirs and other restaurant services.

TRENDS FOR THE '90s

"Expectations, perceptions and reality. The menu creates the expectations and the perceptions. We deliver the reality to meet both. The light-hearted, whimsical menu done in a quality way and used properly can be a terrific sales and marketing tool. Not only does it sell well, it relaxes your customers and puts them in a 'I'm going to enjoy myself' kind of mood."

paper stock
70# Glacier Opaque White

typeface
Lithos, Light & Bold *(body copy)*

printing technique
Offset Lithography

number of color inks
Three

number produced
10,000

restaurant
TGI Friday's

location
Dallas, Texas

design firm
Stafford Ream, Inc.

designer
Ed Stafford

photographers
Scott Metcalf
Ed Stafford

year produced
1993

CONCEPT

The designer's objective was to show food in early morning light, but still maintain Friday's fun feeling.

SPECIAL VISUAL EFFECTS

A combination of painted objects adds a twist to an otherwise straight-ahead food shot.

TRENDS FOR THE '90s

"Desktop publishing."

paper stock
100# NW Gloss *(cover)*

typeface
Novarese

printing technique
Offset Lithography

number of color inks
Four-color Process

number produced
1,500

restaurant
Eat'n Park

location
Pittsburgh, Pennsylvania

design firm
Informing Design

creative director/designer
Robert Firth

CONCEPT

Eat'n Park's menu design emulates their slogan, "The Place for Smiles." The cover design depicts the operation's signature smiley-face cookies lined up in rows.

SPECIAL VISUAL EFFECTS

The designer's interest in trompe l'oeil art gave him the idea of using die-cut plates on the inside of the menu. An actual plate, almost to scale, was used to shoot the inside pages.

paper stock
Teslin *(synthetic)*

printing technique
Die-cut, Laminated

restaurant
J W's Steak House *(Marriott Hotels & Resorts)*

location
nationwide

design firm
Associates Design

art director
Charles Polonsky

designers
Jill Arena
Donna Milerd

illustrator
Donna Milerd

year produced
1993

CONCEPT

Muted colors and a loose abstract style appearing throughout Marriott's J W's Steak House menu covers reflect the restaurant's casual atmosphere. The cleverly designed half-fold pieces contain inside pockets to hold a variety of inserts, granting J W's Steak House the ability to diversify its menu. The imaginative visuals reinforce the theme "food as fun."

SPECIAL VISUAL EFFECTS

Because the insert sheets are printed on vellum, the menu's abstract pattern subtly shows through, adding dimension and depth to the inside of the menu.

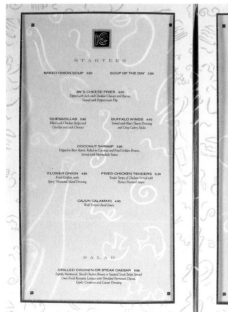

paper stock
French Speckletone *(cover)*
Vellum *(inserts)*

typefaces
Engravers Roman, Univers, Goudy

printing technique
Offset Lithography

number of color inks
Four *(cover)* **Two** *(inside)*

number produced
1,500

restaurant
Copperfield's *(Hilton DFW)*

location
Dallas, Texas

design firm
Associates Design

art director
Charles Polonsky

designer/illustrator
Jill Arena

photographer
stock photography

year produced
1992-93

CONCEPT

Created to depict the Western frontier, Copperfield's menu cover uses layered images to lend depth and provide a contemporary Western feel. The interior of the half-folds features perforated corners and edges for holding insert sheets.

paper stock
12pt Champion Kromecote C1S

typeface
Barcelona

printing technique
Offset Lithography

number of color inks
Four

number produced
1,500

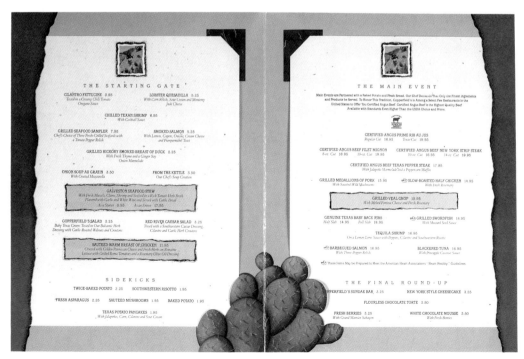

2

Ethnic Menus

restaurant
Golden Temple

location
Brookline, Massachusetts

design firm
Monica Banks & Company

designer/illustrator
Monica Banks

copywriter
Frank Taw

year produced
1993 *("Holiday Cheers" 1992)*

CONCEPT

The menus, T-shirts, and mugs feature mutated fish characters, composed of Chinese foods printed and pieced together. For example, the "Holiday Cheers" mutant has a mushroom cap body, pig's feet, and broccoli antlers. All the mutants have the same fish face.

The menus market the restaurant as a special place to celebrate the holidays indicated. Evocative holiday images are integrated into scenes with the fish mutations. The four mugs were created as gifts for customers on Valentine's Day.

TRENDS FOR THE '90s

"Now that desktop publishing is ubiquitous, restaurant managers and chefs are inclined to change the text of the menus quite often (usually daily). In my experience, they often effect these changes themselves on their computers. It is then the designer's job to provide an effective and powerful context for a word-processed menu by concentrating on the logo, signage, and menu shell, and by providing an intelligently designed typographic menu format to be followed in the restaurant...."

typefaces
Futura Family

printing technique
Offset Lithography

number of color of inks
Two to Four Colors

GOLDEN TEMPLE
Speedy Delivery

GOLDEN TEMPLE
New Year's

GOLDEN TEMPLE
Holiday Cheers

ALWAYS REQUEST

Each selection Golden Temple serves is individually prepared. If you need to make special requests due to diet restrictions (fat, sugar, etc.), please tell us when you place your order.

HEALTHY COOKING

All of our recipes that require cooking oil are prepared with canola oil, which contains no cholesterol and has half the saturated fat content of other vegetable oils.

CALL TODAY FOR

Eat healthy—eat at Golden Temple tonight. Or enjoy the convenience of Golden Temple selections delivered right to your door. Call 277-9722 today.

HEALTHY FOOD

Chinese cooking, with its emphasis on vegetables and starches (especially rice and noodles), is some of the healthiest food you can include in your diet. We strongly encourage you to eat Chinese cuisine often!

CALL 277-9722

FOR DELIVERY FROM
GOLDEN TEMPLE
1651 Beacon Street, Brookline (Washington Square)

APPETIZERS

Barbecued Boneless Ribs 6.75
Barbecued Ribs 6.55
Pork Strips 6.55
Chicken Fingers 6.55
Chicken Wings 4.65
Chicken Livers with Walnuts 5.95
Beef Teriyaki 6.55
Curry Beef Puffs 4.95
Fried Squid (Calamari) 6.95
Fried Scallops 6.95
Fried Shrimps 6.75
Crab Rangoon 5.95
Egg Rolls (2) 3.95
Peking Ravioli 4.55
Scallion Pancake 3.45
Fried Won Tons 3.45

Combination Appetizers

No. 1 Single Egg Roll, Ribs, and Pork Strips 9.75
No. 2 Single Egg Roll, Fried Won Tons, and Chicken Wings 9.75

Special Appetizers

Temple Platter
Egg Roll, Barbecued Ribs, Fried Shrimps, Fried Won Tons, Chicken Wings, and Pork Strips
Serves two. 15.95
Serves three. 23.55

Spicy Ginger Clams
Fresh steamed littleneck clams in a hot, spicy ginger garlic sauce
Small, approx. 12 clams. 12.85
Large, approx. 18 clams. 17.25

Littleneck Clams (Seasonal)
Fresh steamed littleneck clams served in black bean sauce
Small, approx. 12 clams. 10.85
Large, approx. 18 clams. 15.25

Shrimp Glazed Tofu
Tofu glazed with shrimp paste and Chinese herbs and spices and lightly stirfried. 4.25

Shao-Mai
Light steamed, open-faced dumplings, stuffed with finely chopped shrimp, pork, water chestnuts, scallions and Chinese seasonings. 5.75

Golden Temple Chicken Wings
Chicken wings delicately prepared in a tangy spicy hot sauce. 6.45

New dish
Spicy hot

Wrapped Shrimps (4)
Large whole shrimps wrapped with bacon and panfried. Served with a special chili sauce and Chinese seasonings. 12.95

Golden Temple Ribs
Large, specially-cut pork ribs in our own barbecue sauce. 13.95

Ribs in Black Bean Sauce
Bite-sized ribs served in black bean sauce. 8.75

SOUPS

Won Ton Soup 2.45
Chicken Won Ton Soup 2.55
Golden Temple Won Ton Soup
Finely chopped pork, water chestnuts and spices wrapped in square won ton noodles in a broth with vegetables and noodles. 4.25
Shrimp Chow Foon Soup
Shrimps, black mushrooms and chow foon noodles in a light broth with vegetables. 4.75
Chicken Rice Soup 2.45
Chicken Yatka Mein Soup 2.55
Roast Pork Yatka Mein Soup 2.45
ToFu Vegetable Soup 2.45
Vegetable Soup 2.45
Egg Drop Soup 2.25
Hot and Sour Soup 2.45

金蘭廣

BEFORE ORDERING YOUR MEAL

Especially for those people who are on diets and health foods: All dishes are cooked to order, therefore we can prepare any dish to your specifications. If for any reason you cannot eat certain ingredients such as cornstarch, M.S.G., oil, salt or sugar, please let us know when ordering.

Any order not listed can be served upon request. Please feel free to request a manager to assist you.

Please pay your server with cash, Mastercard, Visa, or The American Express © Card. The omission of personal checks is intentional. Delivery available at an additional charge, please call for information: 277-9722

GOLDEN TEMPLE
Father's Day

restaurant
Ciao Mein *(The Hyatt Regency)*

location
Irvine, California

design firm
The Front

designer
Mehdi Rafaty

copywriter
Hans Desai

year produced
1992

CONCEPT

Ciao Mein's menu reflects two different cultures, Italian and Chinese, but like the restaurant, is not typical of either. The cover of the menu is made of chipboard which has been made visually appealing and resilient through a special pigmentation process. The pigmentation gives the menu hues of gold, bronze and green, and at the same time makes it almost waterproof. The inside pages are made of a plastic material and treated the same way.

The insert pages fit through a laser printer, which allows the restaurateur flexibility to change menu selections. The staff simply make the changes to the pages on an in-house computer. The pages are then tinted. Three screws hold the menu pages together and allow new pages to be easily inserted.

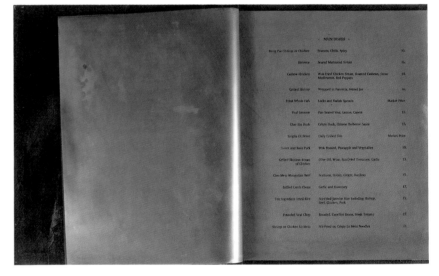

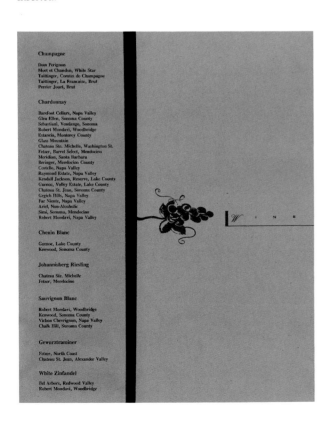

paper stock
Duralene

typeface
Bitstream Amerigo

printing technique
Laser-printed

number of color inks
Four

number produced
150

design budget
$5,000

CROSSROADS

restaurant
Crossroads

location
Charlotte, North Carolina

design firm
Metro Media Arts & Communication

designers
Dan McClerin
Sharon Tallent

copywriters
Sharon Tallent
Kip McKlerin

year produced
1992

CONCEPT

Crossroads' menu can be easily revised, allowing the restaurant to promote holidays, live music and special events. The daily menu is printed in-house and inserted into the cover with spray adhesive. This format is relatively inexpensive, so guests have the opportunity to take menus home, as many do. This is a very personal way to help promote the restaurant.

SPECIAL EFFECTS

The front cover artwork is an original photo of a rare map entitled *America Septentrionalis*. The photo illustrates the region from which the restaurant draws inspiration, and links the present back to the colonial period upon which many of their preparations are based.

TRENDS FOR THE '90s

"Our clientele appreciate a greater awareness of our products and preparations. Not only do we communicate our concept, but our authenticity. Our menu helps to ignite this philosophy, and as a consequence, our guests feel more confident in their decision to share their dining experience with us...."

paper stock
Recycled

typeface
Bembo

printing technique
Offset Lithography

number of color inks
Four

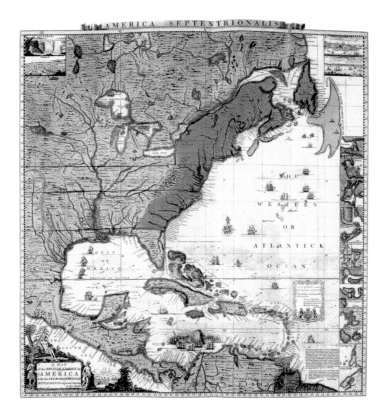

AFTER DINNER

Cappicino Frozen Souffle
With A Chocolate Covered Coffee Bean & Cinnamon

Peanut Butter-Chocolate Chip Cheesecake
New York Style with Graham Crust

Fresh Florida Grapefruit Sorbet
Served in an Orange Chalupa Cup with Berry Couli

Triple Chocolate Crepes
*Cocoa Crepe Filled with Whipped Ghirardelli Chocolate & Cinnamon
Served on Mocha Creme Anglais*

Strawberry Sundae
With Homemade Strawberry Ice Cream & Pecan Sandies

Fresh Gaffney Peach Cobbler
Baked Homestyle & Served with Velvet Sassafrass Sauce

Three Dollars and Ninety-Five

New World Coffees

Guatemala Espresso, Costa Rican Regular & Decafe
Press Brewed at Your Table
Three Dollars

Crossroads Coffee
Custom Blended with Beans Exclusively from Southern America
One Dollar

Dessert Wines *By The Glass*	Port *By The Glass*
Bonny Doon Framboise *Five Fifty*	Rutherford Hill *Five Dollars*
Muscat Canelli *Four Fifty*	Warres Grand Reserve '63 *Ten Dollars*
Sweet Sherries *By The Glass*	Cockburn's Tawny '73 *Eight Dollars*
Sandaman's Characters (Olo Roso) *Six Dollars*	Dow's Boardroom Tawny '78 *Six Dollars*
Gonzales Nectar Cream *Six Dollars*	

Chef Kip McClerin
Kelly Estes

restaurant
Bondini

location
New York, New York

design firm
PM Design & Marketing

designer
Philip Marzo

year produced
1993

CONCEPT

To update and unify Bondini's somewhat
scattered graphic identity, and to convey
the restaurant's classic Italian cuisine and
relaxed, sophisticated atmosphere, the
designer provided an artichoke image.
The menu's artichoke image, along with its
fresh combination of antique typefaces
and recycled paper stock, proves this
established restaurant as a place worth
rediscovering.

TRENDS FOR THE '90s

"Menus...will function beyond listing food
and beverages. As a marketing tool,
menus will increasingly function as a bill-
board for added values...that customers
have come to expect. The challenge is for
restaurants and graphic designers to create
simple, well-organized and very usable
menus with compelling, visual appeal."

typefaces
Coronet Bold, Lilth

number of color inks
Two

number produced
300

design budget
Under $3,000

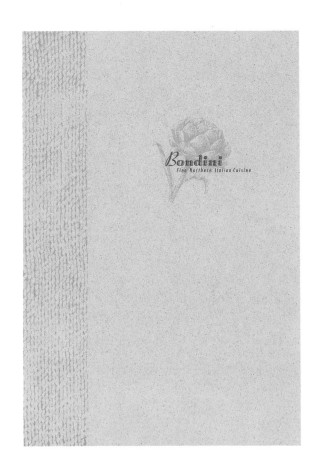

Bondini

Bar Menu

BRUSCHETTA
Grilled Bread topped with Tomatoes and Argula...$5.00

VONGOLE AL FORNO
Baked Clams with Oregano...$7.00

FOCACCIA CON MOZZARELLA
Served with Sundried Tomatoes...$6.50

RADICCHIO EN CARROZZA
Spicy Sandwich of Mozzarella between Radicchio Leaves...$6.00

CALAMARI FRITTI
Fried Squid served with Red Pepper Puree...$6.50

PHILLEO

38

CAFÉ RESTAURANT

la Gauloise

502 6th Avenue
New York, NY 10011
212 · 691 1363

restaurant
La Gauloise

location
New York, New York

art director
Isabella von Buol

designer/illustrator
Isabella von Buol

copywriter
Jean Robert de Cavel

year produced
1993

CONCEPT

La Gauloise translated means 'the Gallic woman.' The menu for this restaurant is expressed by a rural-like floral pattern. The richness of the colors refers to turn-of-the-century France.

SPECIAL VISUAL EFFECTS

The rooster is a symbol for France and its cuisine, and is used to convey some of the playfulness and wit of the French. The dessert menu is influenced by a fairy-tale, dreamlike atmosphere with the symbol of the little baker boy as an additional touch.

TRENDS FOR THE '90s

"The trend in the '90s will definitely lead to the menu not just as a statement of variety of foods but as a means to express the personality of the restaurant. The menu will be used to communicate the character of the food served and become an active marketing tool. Diversity, uniqueness and originality are terms that replace the ever-exchangeable menu."

paper stock
Strathmore Beau Brilliant

typefaces
Garamond, Old Century Book

printing technique
Offset Lithography

number produced
2,000

design budget
$4,500

restaurant
Hemispheres *(The Hyatt Orlando Airport)*

location
Orlando, Florida

design firm
Associates Design

art director
Charles Polonsky

designers
Roberta Serafini
Donna Sommerville
Jill Arena

illustrator
Roberta Serafini

year produced
1992-1993

CONCEPT

Hemispheres' hard-covered menu is both sturdy and unique, with interior corner pockets to hold insert sheets. Embossed vertical stripes enhance and add texture to the black leather cover.

SPECIAL VISUAL EFFECTS

The two-color insert sheets each possess a half-tone of textured paper to provide a background pattern, and a half-tone of a portion of the cover illustration to display visual continuity throughout the menu. The rich toned four-color illustration was printed and die-cut as a sticker, and placed on each cover.

paper stock
Leather

typeface
Burlington Open

printing technique
Offset Lithography

number of color inks
Four *(cover)* **Two** *(inside)*

number produced
750

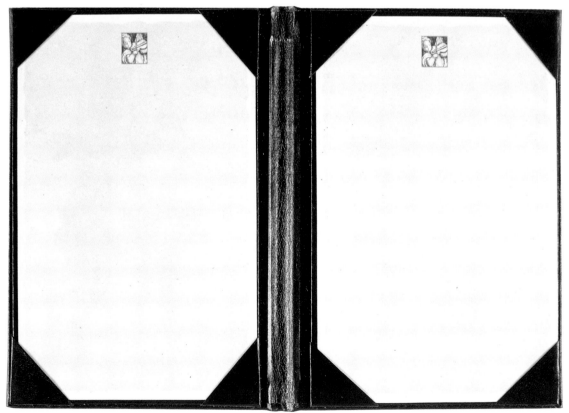

restaurant
Prima Sixth Avenue Grill

location
Carmel, California

design firm
Jim Moon Designs

designer
Jim Moon

year produced
1993

CONCEPT

Originally, Prima was conceived of as a coffee specialty property with a high-tech Italian look. When an excellent restaurant property came available in Carmel, Prima Sixth Avenue Grill was born. The logo was modified and the high-tech Italian look adapted to form the theme of the restaurant. Prima hasn't abandoned its original character—specialty coffees are still sold at the coffee counter.

SPECIAL VISUAL EFFECTS

In addition to the logo, individual coffee beans are employed to show different blends and varietals.

paper stock
B 100 Vintage Gloss Cover

typefaces
Calligraphy, Parisian

printing technique
Offset Lithography

number of color inks
Three

number produced
5,000

design budget
$7,500

41

restaurant
Tosca

location
Hingham, Massachusetts

designer/illustrator
Marie Flaherty

copywriters
Patricia Kane
Paul Kanavan

logo design
Niemitz Designs

year produced
1993

CONCEPT

Plastic covers and sheets edged in black give Tosca a flexible format for their menus, allowing these menus to easily change seasonally, and eventually, weekly and even daily.

SPECIAL VISUAL EFFECTS

Both the menus and collateral were designed to reflect the rustic natural atmosphere of Tosca's newly renovated 1910 Granary building. Architectural and design elements of the restaurant, such as the arches in the main structure, windows and doorways, are used in the menu. The texture of the paper stock is reminiscent of the cone-shaped lighting fixtures that hang over the length of the bar.

typefaces
Caslon Condensed
Futura Condensed
Tekton *(fall and winter, and updated menu)*

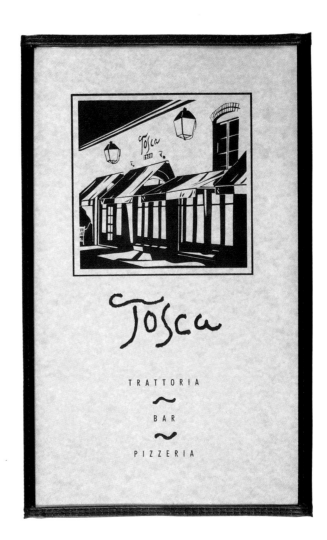

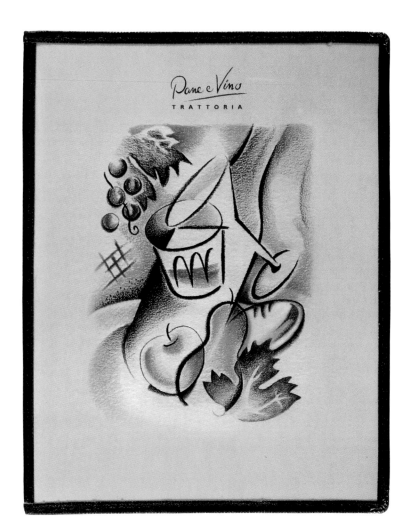

restaurant
Pane e Vino

location
Los Angeles, California

design firm
Rod Dyer Group

art director/designer
Rod Dyer

illustrator
John Sabel

year produced
1993

CONCEPT

Pane e Vino's menu cover has a bright festive image, designed to convey the restaurant's ambiance and feeling.

TRENDS FOR THE '90s

"We do all our printing with a computer including the color laser."

paper stock
French Speckletone Chalk

typeface
Garamond

printing technique
Color Laser

number of color inks
Full-color

number produced
200

design budget
$500

43

restaurant
Bistro Roti

location
San Francisco, California

designer
Michael Mabry

year produced
1993

CONCEPT

Bistro Roti's menu is designed to reflect a French bistro style, at the same time incorporating elements of San Francisco and a "casual" look. The orange color was used to flatter the customer.

SPECIAL EFFECTS

The "Plats du Jour" insert was intended to look casual and not too well integrated into the otherwise well-defined graphics.

TRENDS FOR THE '90s

Menus will "...most likely (be) changeable from day to day or week to week."

paper stock
120# Springhill Index Ivory

typefaces
Various

printing technique
Offset Lithography

number of color inks
Four

number produced
5,000

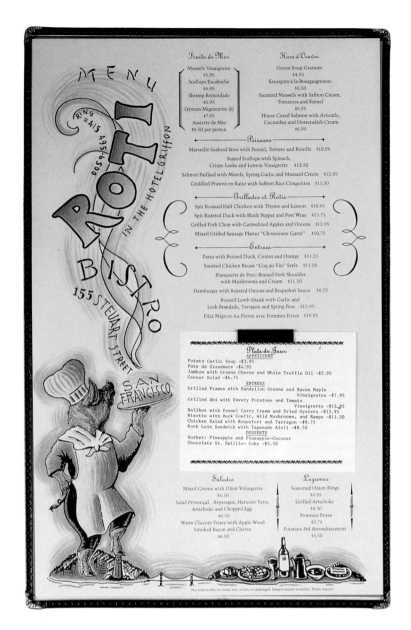

restaurant
Spazzo

location
Bellevue, Washington

design firm
Tim Girvin Design, Inc.

art director
Laurie Vette

designer
Maria Mason

illustrator
Tim Girvin

copywriter
Ted Furst

year produced
1992

CONCEPT

Spazzo's theme is Mediterranean with an upbeat and lively palette. A fairly complex illustrative unit was created that includes both a playful typographic design and an intermingling of a series of drawn elements used throughout the restaurant in architectural signing and other applications.

SPECIAL VISUAL EFFECTS

Overlays created on Japanese and Italian handmade paper give the menu a kind of multi-dimensional quality, expanded upon in the use of water imagery in other parts of the collateral.

TRENDS FOR THE '90s

"Menus, no doubt, shall continue their upward swing towards unique forms of visual/theatrical presentation, and designers will have a continued presence in expressing this. My sense is that there will be an increasing expansion of the digital application for design development, but my opinion (like that of Mr. M. Glaser) is to retain the spirit of original tools, that of the brush loaded with pigment caressing the surface of a roughened, handmade paper to capture a certain effect...."

paper stock
Simpson Evergreen

typefaces
Charlemagne, Futura

printing process
Offset Lithography

number of color inks
Five PMS

number produced
2,000

design budget
$8,500

MEDITERRANEAN
GRILL

KRISTY LINDGREEN OF TIM GIRVIN DESIGN, INC.

KRISTY LINDGREEN OF TIM GIRVIN DESIGN, INC.

restaurant
Altezzo

location
Tacoma, Washington

design firm
The Menu Workshop

designers
Liz Kearney
Margo Christianson

illustrator
Debbie Hanley

copywriters
Steve Tischler
Altezzo
The Menu Workshop

year produced
1993

CONCEPT

Altezzo, which means 'height' in Italian, is located on the top floor of the Sheraton Hotel in Tacoma. The menu program was part of a complete overhaul of the restaurant. A formal Continental dining room was transformed into an Italian bistro that focuses on value and family-style service. Italian murals, trompe l'oeil finishes and a three-dimensional sandblasted sign of the logo lit from above complete the interior design.

The menu has a classy, clean, simple design with a rustic, lively scratchboard illustration. The dinner menu has die-cut pockets to hold fresh sheets which change nightly. The wine list and dessert menu also have the same flexibility and menu cords which hold fresh sheets in place. Die-cut edged business cards complete the program.

paper stock
Classic Crest Recycled

typefaces
Copperplate, Futura

printing technique
Offset Lithography

number of color inks
Two

COGNACS

Courvoisier VS	4.75
Courvoisier VSOP	6.50
Hennessey VS	4.50
Hennessey VSOP	5.25
Hennessey XO	10.50
Martell Cordon Bleu	6.50
Remy Martin VSOP	5.25
Remy Martin Napoleon	8.25

CORDIALS / LIQUEURS

Amaretto di Sarrano	4.25
Baileys Irish Cream	4.00
B & B	4.25
Drambuie	4.50
Frangelico	4.25
Grand Marnier	4.50
Sambucca	3.75
Tia Maria	3.75
Tuaca	4.50

PORTS

Fonseca 1977	15.00
Graham's LBV 1986	5.00
Sandeman Founders Rsv.	4.50

GRAPPA

House Flavored	5.50
Mastroberadino Taurasi	7.00
Mezza Coroma	5.00

DESSERT WINE

Chateau Rieussec	5.00
J. Phelps L.H. Riesling	4.50
Quady Essencia Orange Muscat	4.00

DESSERTS

TIRAMISU
espresso and rum soaked ladyfingers
layered with mascarpone cheese
3.75

SEMIFREDDO
vanilla ice cream with shot of espresso
and whipped cream
3.25

TORTA di LIMONE
lemon tart
3.75

FRUTTA del GIORNO
fresh seasonal fruit
3.50

TORTA di CIOCCOLATO
flourless chocolate mousse cake
with white chocolate cream anglaise
3.95

GRANITA del GIORNO
today's Italian ice
2.95

ABOUT ALTEZZO

IN ITALY, LOVE OF FOOD AND WINE IS SYNONYMOUS WITH LIFE ITSELF. IN KEEPING WITH TRADITION, WE AT ALTEZZO BELIEVE WE HAVE CREATED THE PERFECT MARRIAGE OF GREAT FOOD AND FINE WINE. THIS IS WHY WE INSIST ON USING ONLY THE FRESHEST HERBS, SEAFOOD AND LOCAL INGREDIENTS.

ALTEZZO IS THE ITALIAN WORD FOR HEIGHT, WHICH IS THE PERFECT NAME FOR A RESTAURANT WITH A SETTING LIKE OURS. SO WHILE YOU'RE TAKING IN OUR PANORAMIC VIEW OF COMMENCEMENT BAY AND MT. RAINIER, RELAX AND ENJOY THE HEIGHT OF ITALIAN CUISINE.

MAKE DINNER AT ALTEZZO A TRADITION.

PRIMI PIATTI

BRUSCHETTA grilled bread with herbed goat cheese, roasted peppers and tomatoes with basil and garlic 3.95
CALAMARI FRITTI deep fried calamari with marinara and lemon aioli 4.95
SALSICCE e PEPERONI sausage and peppers with parmesan roasted garlic polenta 4.50
MOZZARELLA CAPRESE fresh mozzarella with roma tomatoes, basil and balsamic vinegar 4.95
COZZE SALTATE sauteed mussels with olive oil, garlic, hot peppers and tomato filets 5.95
ANTIPASTO MISTO chef's selection of italian appetizers 6.95

ZUPPA e INSALATA

ZUPPA del GIORNO today's soup 2.95
INSALATA MISTA mixed garden greens with fried onions and kalamata olive vinaigrette 3.50
INSALATA di VERDURA alla GRIGLIA mixed grilled vegetables with balsamic vinegar and virgin olive oil 3.75
INSALATA CESARE classic whole leaf caesar salad with roasted garlic croutons and shaved parmesan 3.95

PIZZA

PIZZA MARGHERITA basil, roma tomatoes and mozzarella 6.95
PIZZA SALSICCE sausage, tomatoes, hot peppers and fontina 7.95
PIZZA PEPERONI toasted red and anaheim peppers, red onion, tomatoes and mozzarella 7.50
PIZZA PROSCIUTTO prosciutto, arugula, parmesan and virgin olive oil 8.50
PIZZA FUNGHI e CIPOLLE assorted mushrooms, carmelized onions, rosemary and fresh mozzarella 8.95
CALZONE di POLLO smoked chicken, marinara, fontina and mozzarella in folded pizza dough 8.75

PASTA

CAPPELLINI al POMODORO angel hair pasta with roma tomatoes, garlic and basil 7.95
LINGUINE con FRUTTI di MARE narrow pasta with mussels, clams, scallops, tomatoes and herbs 9.95
RAVIOLI di GRANCHIO crab filled ravioli with carmelized shallots, parsley, red peppers and pinenuts 10.50
FETTUCCINE alla PANNA wide pasta with asparagus, peas, basil, cream and romano cheese 8.50
LINGUINE CARRETIERA narrow pasta with shiitake mushrooms, tomatoes, cream, hot peppers and vodka 8.95
PENNE con POLLO AFFUMICATO tubular pasta with smoked chicken, olives, onions and pecorino cheese 9.50
CAVATAPPI con SALSICCE e BROCCOLI corkscrew pasta with sausage, broccoli, tomatoes and ricotta cheese 8.50

CARNE, POLLAME e PESCE

PESCE del GIORNO today's fresh fish market price
MEZZO POLLO GRIGLIATO grilled boneless half chicken with onions, garlic, crushed red pepper and virgin olive oil 9.95
PETTI di POLLO ARROSTO mozzarella and parsley stuffed breast of chicken with pancetta and white wine sauce 10.50
BISTECCA con FUNGHI e PREZZEMOLO grilled t-bone steak with sauteed mushrooms, pepper and parsley oils 14.95
COTOLETTA d'AGNELLO alla GRIGLIA grilled lamb chops with roasted eggplant, mint, lemon and virgin olive oil 14.50
SCALLOPINE di VITELLO veal scallopine sauteed with sweet peppers, mushrooms, herbs and white wine 13.50
GRIGLIATO MISTO di FRUTTI di MARE mixed grill of salmon, mussels and prawns with a smoked tomato sauce 14.95

LA FAMIGLIA

served for two or more family style

entrees come with choice of soup or mixed green salad
and includes choice of tiramisu or granita for dessert

CIOPPINO dungeness crab, prawns, calamari, mussels, clams and fresh fish in a tomato-red wine broth
14.95 per person

RIGATONI con SUGO BOLOGNESE e BESCIAMELLA large tubular pasta baked with meat and cream sauces
14.95 per person

POLLO ARROSTO alla CASALINGA roasted chicken in a tomato, olive and pepper sauce served over linguine pasta
15.95 per person

MISTO CARNE alla GRIGLIA mixed grill of sausage, lamb and chicken with mushrooms, tomatoes and onions over soft polenta
17.95 per person

chef Charlie McManus

CHARLIE McMANUS
CHEF

1320 BROADWAY PLAZA, 26TH FLOOR
TACOMA, WASHINGTON 98402

206.591.4155

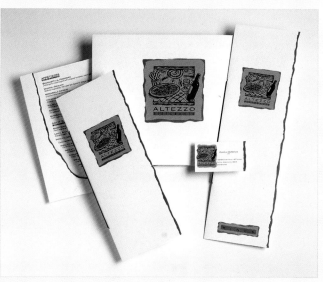

47

restaurant
Le Boulanger

location
Santa Clara, California

design firm
THARP DID IT

designers
Rick Tharp
Jean Mogannam
Jana Heer

illustrators
Kelly O'Connor
Rick Tharp

year produced
1991

CONCEPT

The identity of a number of Le Boulanger owner-operated bakeries was updated through the use of this new hand-drawn logotype. An emblem was created around the logotype to be used on packaging and labels. A custom stencil typeface based on Universal was also created.

TRENDS FOR THE '90s

"I do not think there are trends with regard to menu design. Look at the number of restaurants on the planet. 'Trends schmends.' Just do what works. There are too many different types of restaurants to be that specific."

typeface
Hand-drawn typefaces

48

restaurant
Mandarin House

location
St. Louis, Missouri

design firm
Purple Seal Graphics

designers
Lim Ho Yen
Andrew G. Dyer

illustrator/copywriter
Lim Ho Yen

year produced
1991

CONCEPT

Images of ancient Chinese pictograms of different ceremonial dining utensils signify the rich history of Chinese culinary art and the fine dining atmosphere at the Mandarin House restaurant. Purple and gold are the restaurant's house colors.

SPECIAL VISUAL EFFECTS

Screened back images.

TRENDS FOR THE '90s

"As more and more people become more environmentally conscious, the menu will be printed on recycled stock with soy-based ink."

paper stock
Curtis Tuscan Terra Flax

typefaces
Futura Condensed
Garamond Condensed

number of color inks
Two

printing techniques
Silkscreen *(cover)*
Offset Lithography *(pages)*

number produced
500

design budget
$2,000

Mandarin House

京園

FINE
CHINESE
CUISINE

St. Louis Union Station / 104 • 106 Street @ Market • 314 • 621 • 6888

MANDARIN HOUSE SPECIALTIES

干貝牛肉	Szechuan Beef and Sea Scallops	9.95
雞牛蝦仁	Beef Chicken and Shrimp Special	9.95
京園蝦仁	Mandarin Shrimp	9.95
	Lightly fried shrimp covered with Szechuan sauce	
京園雞	Mandarin Chicken	7.95
	Marinated chicken then fried to golden brown	
白菜冬菇	Chinese Vegetables with Black Mushrooms	7.95
紅燒干貝	Hong Shao Sea Scallops	9.95
	Sautéed with peas and carrots in a hot savory sauce	
脆皮鴨	Crispy Duck	9.95
龍蝦尾	Lobster Tails	Seasonal
	Sautéed in our special Mandarin sauce or spicy Szechuan sauce	
清蒸魚	Steamed Fish (Whole Fish)	Seasonal
	Seasonal selection steamed to your likeness	
宮爆牛肉	Kung Pao Beef	8.95
	Sliced beef and vegetables with Kung Pao sauce	
陳皮牛	Orange Flavored Beef	8.95
回鍋肉	Double-Sautéed Pork	7.95
	Sliced barbecued pork, sautéed with cabbage and bamboo shoots	

FRIED RICE and CHOW MEIN (FRIED NOODLES)

京園炒飯	Mandarin Fried Rice	7.25
	Shrimp, pork, chicken	
海鮮炒飯	Seafood Fried Rice	8.25
	Scallop, shrimp, crab meat	
蝦仁炒飯	Shrimp Fried Rice	6.95
雞球炒飯	Chicken Fried Rice	6.25
叉燒炒飯	Pork Fried Rice	6.25
白飯	Steamed Rice (one serving)	1.00
京園炒麵	Mandarin Chow Mein	6.95
	Shrimp, beef, chicken, pork	
雞肉炒麵	Chicken Chow Mein	6.25
牛肉炒麵	Beef Chow Mein	6.25
蝦仁炒麵	Shrimp Chow Mein	6.95

SEAFOOD

乾燒魚	Hot Braised Fish	Seasonal
	Finely chopped water chestnuts, mushrooms, bamboo shoots with hot pepper sauce	
狗餃魚	Sweet and Sour Fish	Seasonal
蝦甜柳	Shrimp with Lobster Sauce	9.75
	Fresh shrimps with egg and scallops, bamboo shoots, water chestnuts, mushrooms and green peas	
狗餃蝦	Sweet and Sour Shrimp	9.75
雪豆蝦	Snow Peas Shrimp	9.75
炒三鮮	Three Ingredients	10.95
	Abalone, shrimp, sea scallops delicately blended, sautéed with snow peas and bamboo shoots	
全家福	Sautéed Happy Family	10.95
	Eight delicacies' Sautéed sea foods and vegetables	
宮爆蝦	Hot Braised Shrimp	9.95
	Lightly fried shrimp blended with our special hot sauce	
宮爆墨魚	Spiced Fried Squid	9.75
木須蝦仁	Mo Shu Shrimp	10.95
魚香蝦	Yu Xan Shrimp	9.75
素菜蝦仁	Shrimp and Vegetables	9.95
	Shrimp, snow peas and water chestnuts	

NOODLES

海鮮炒麵	Mandarin Special Noodles	10.95
	Shrimp, Sea Scallops, Beef, Black Mushrooms and vegetables stir fried with soft noodles	
牛炒麵	Beef Noodles	8.75
雞炒麵	Chicken Noodles	8.25
蝦炒麵	Shrimp Noodles	9.25
叉燒麵	B-B-Q Pork Noodles	8.25
炒碼麵	Combination Soup Noodles	8.75
	Shrimp, Sea Scallops, Black Mushrooms and Vegetables in Chicken broth	

According to Chinese legend, noodles are a symbol of longevity

Spicy Hot

Spicy Hot

restaurant
Phuket Thai Restaurant

location
Atlanta, Georgia

design firm
Axis Design Associates, Inc.

designer
Martin Villarreal

illustrator
Rebecca Perera

photographer
Dianne Fiumara

year produced
1993

CONCEPT

The menu covers of the adult-oriented Phuket Thai Restaurant were handmade in Germany. The colors and the bamboo illustrations are coordinated to match the interior decor of the restaurant.

SPECIAL VISUAL EFFECTS

The cover photograph is of a temple in Bangkok. The die-cut opening gives the feeling of entering. The bamboo in the menu matches the green bamboo in the restaurant itself.

TRENDS FOR THE '90s

"I believe the trend of menu design for the '90s will be...modern...with a Western flair since most design trends for this country tend to start on the West Coast."

paper stock
Beckett Cambric Colonial White

typefaces
Goudy, Calligraphy

printing technique
Offset Lithography

number of color inks
Two

number produced
300

design budget
$900

Appetizers

CHAU KAO	7.25
Combination shrimp, satay, poa pia, and kratong thong.	
BAMBOO SHRIMP	4.95
Shrimp wrapped in wonton skin, fried, and served with house special sauce.	
PHUKET ROLLS	4.95
Minced pork, crab meat, wrapped in dried tofu skin, deep fried.	
SATAY	4.95
Broiled pork or chicken in spices, peanut sauce with cucumber salad.	
MEE KROB	4.95
Fried rice noodle with mixture of pork, shrimp, green onion.	
KRATONG THONG	3.95
Royal Hors d'Oeuvre with minced meat and coconut cream.	
POA PIA	3.95
Pork, bean thread, black mushroom, stuffed in eggroll, with sauce.	

Soup

TOM YUM		6.25
Shrimp soup with mushrooms, lemon grass, lime juice, and hot pepper.		
PO TAR		8.95
Sea food combo in hot pot.		
TOM KHA		6.25
Sliced breast of chicken soup, coconut milk, lime juice, and hot pepper.		
WON TON SOU	Sm. 2.00	Lg. 5.00
TOFU SOUP	Sm. 2.00	Lg. 5.00

Yum

YUM YAI SALAD	4.95
Fresh tossed salad with chicken, shrimp, in house sweet and sour dressing.	
CHAU SUAN SALAD	4.95
Tossed salad with Phuket dressing.	
YUM KUN CHIANG	4.95
Browned sausage in hot spices and lime juice.	
YUM WOON SEN	4.95
Shrimp, ground pork, bean thread, in hot spicy sauce.	
LARB	5.95
Ground beef in hot spices, lime juice.	
NAM TOK	5.95
Sliced beef in hot spices, lime juice.	
YUM GOONG	5.95
Shrimp sauteed with lime juice, hot chili pepper.	
PHUKET YUM	6.95
Shrimp, scallops, and squid in hot spices and lime juice.	

Chicken

CHICKEN CASHEW NUT	6.95
Sauteed sliced chicken with onions, mushrooms, scallions, and roasted cashew nuts.	
CHICKEN CURRY	6.95
Chicken cooked with coconut milk, red curry, and vegetable.	
BASIL CHICKEN	6.95
Sauteed chicken with basil and chili pepper.	
GINGER CHICKEN	6.95
Chicken cooked with black mushrooms, scallions, and ginger.	
CHICKEN AND MUSHROOMS	6.95
Chicken stir fried with mushrooms.	
PAN FRIED CHICKEN	7.95
Breaded chicken marinated with special sauce, with mixed vegetables, served in hot plate.	

Duck

PHUKET DUCK	7.95
House roast duck, Thai style, boneless, topped with brown sauce and vegetable.	
PED NAM DANG	7.95
Roast duck on vegetables, prepared in red curry sauce.	
GINGER DUCK	7.95
Duck stir-fried with ginger, black mushroom, and vegetables.	
DUCK CURRY	7.95
Curried duck cooked in coconut milk, with bamboo shoots.	

Pork

GARLIC PORK	6.95
Pork with garlic and black pepper.	
PORK AND PEPPER CORN	6.95
Pork cooked in hot spicy sauce and green pepper corn.	
SPICY PORK	6.95
Pork cooked with Thai spices and green bean.	

Beef

BEEF CURRY	6.95
Beef cooked with coconut milk and Thai vegetables.	
BEEF WITH OYSTER SAUCE	6.95
Beef in oyster sauce with vegetable.	
BEEF PUD KEE MAO	6.95
Hot spicy sauteed beef with chili sauce.	
GARLIC BEEF	6.95
Beef with garlic and black pepper.	

50

restaurant
Imari *(The Tokyo Hilton)*

location
Tokyo, Japan

design firm
Design Resource

designer
Mari Makinami

illustrator
Yoshiharo Honda

copywriter
The Tokyo Hilton

year produced
1991

CONCEPT
Imari is a village in Saga prefecture, on the Southern Japanese island of Kyushu, where the famous Imari pottery and chinaware is produced and shipped to places all over the world. The menu design is associated with the restaurant's name.

SPECIAL VISUAL EFFECTS
A unique flower design pattern with typical colors such as red, blue, shiny white and gold have been used, as they often appear on the original chinaware and pottery.

TRENDS FOR THE '90s
"In Japan, Western designs were rather elegant and gorgeous. In the future it will be much more simple and straight-forward, changing on a monthly or seasonal basis with the help of in-house print shops and office desktop printing equipment. Traditional Japanese restaurants, however, remain to be very different and particular in their styles of menu design."

paper stock
Foil Paper

typeface
Century

printing technique
Offset Lithography with Coating

number of color inks
Six Custom Colors, Gold Hot Stamp

number produced
100

design budget
$800,000

前 菜
APPETIZERS

ツナのミルフィーユ わさびクリーム
Tuna Mille Feuille with Potato Crisp, Wasabi Cream and Avocado Relish ········· ¥1,800

フォアグラとチキンのグールマンディーズ
Gourmandise of Goose Liver with Chicken and French Cepe Mushrooms ········· ¥2,500

サーモンの"たたき" 和風ドレッシング
Marinated Salmon with Black Pepper and Soya Vinaigrette ········· ¥1,500

帆立貝のカルパチョ ハーブドレッシング
Carpaccio of Fresh Scallop in Herb Dressing with Crisp Greens ········· ¥1,800

スコットランド産スモークサーモン
Smoked Scotch Salmon with Condiments ········· ¥2,400

シーフードの温製サラダ バジルビネグレット
Warm Seafood Salad with Basil Vinaigretta ········· ¥1,500

グリーンアスパラガスとパルマハム
Fresh Asparagus with Parma Ham ········· ¥1,900

小海老のラビオリ トマトバジルソース
Shrimp Ravioli with Tomato Basil Sauce ········· ¥1,900

エスカルゴ "シャブリジェンヌ"
Baked Escargots with Chablis Herb Butter ········· ¥1,900

スープ
SOUP

本日のコンソメ 温製又は冷製
Hot or Chilled Consomme ········· ¥950

フレンチ オニオン スープ
Baked French Onion Soup ········· ¥1,100

冷製ポテトスープ "ビシソワーズ"
Chilled Vishyssoise ········· ¥950

クレイフィッシュビスク コニャック風味
Crayfish Cream Soup with Cognac and Scallop Dumplings ········· ¥1,200

サラダ
SALADS

シーザーサラダ
Caesar's Salad ········· ¥1,400

季節のミックスサラダ
Mixed Seasonal Salad ········· ¥1,000

トマトサラダ オニオンとパセリ添え
Sliced Tomatoes with Onions ········· ¥1,000

キューカンバーサラダ ディル風味
Cucumber with Dill Yoghurt ········· ¥1,000

アボカドとグレープフルーツサラダ
Avocado Grapefruit Salad with Basil Dressing ········· ¥1,200

チーズ、デザート、アイスクリームはワゴンからどうぞ
Cheese, Desserts and Ice Cream from the Trolley

Prices plus 10% service charge are subject to 3% consumption and 3% local excise taxes.

魚介料理
SEAFOOD

帆立貝と車海老のソテー シャンパンキャビアバター
Sauteed Scallops and Prawns
with Champagne and Caviar Butter, Creamed Potatoes with Crisp Onions ········· ¥2,800

帆立貝のグリルと小海老のラビオリ トマトバジルバター
Grilled Scallops with Shrimp Ravioli in Tomato Basil Butter ········· ¥2,800

サーモンの網焼きとマッシュルームリゾット スパイシーピメントバター
Broiled Salmon on Mushroom Risotto with Spicy Pimento Butter ········· ¥3,100

サーモンのステーキ クレイフィッシュコニャックバター
Salmon Steak with Crayfish Cognac Butter, Creamed Potatoes with Onions ········· ¥3,100

めかじきのステーキ スパイシーチリバター
Seared Swordfish Steak with Spicy Chill Butter, Herb Potatoes and Creamed Spinach ········· ¥2,400

ツナのロースト ポートワインソース
Roasted Tuna with Bacon in a Clam Sauce with Port, Creamed Potatoes with Onions ········· ¥2,700

車海老のグリル ハラペニャピメントソース
Grilled Marinated Prawns with Jalapena Pimento Sauce
Mushroom Risotto and Leaf Spinach ········· ¥3,100

鯛のマリネ 和風マスタードソースバルサミコ風味
Marinated Fillet of Dory with Stirfried Vegetables in Balsamic Soya Mustard Butter ········· ¥2,400

メインコース
MAIN COURSE

若鶏のグリル スパイシーソース
Grilled Devilled Chicken with Country Hashed Potatoes and Creamed Spinach ········· ¥2,900

ローストラムチョップ ガーリックソース
Roasted Lamb Chops
with Blanched Garlic and Ratatouille, Gratined Potatoes with Thyme and Green Beans ········· ¥3,100

仔羊のフィレ肉 マスタードソース
Roasted Fillet of Lamb
with Mustard Sauce, Creamed Hashed Potatoes and Green Beans ········· ¥3,100

鴨のロースト ナチュラルソース
Crisp Roasted Duck
with Natural Jus, Creamed Hashed Potatoes, Sauteed Cabbage ········· ¥2,900

仔牛のエスカロープ ラズベリー風味ポートワインソース
Escalopes of Veal with Green Peppercorns in a Raspberry Flavoured Port Wine Sauce
with Crisp Rice Cakes ········· ¥3,100

鴨とフォアグラのタルト スウィートシェリークリーム
Baked Duck Tart with Goose Liver and Sweet Sherry Cream ········· ¥2,900

リブアイステーキのグリル レッドオニオンバター
Grilled Ribeye Steak
with Red Onion Butter, Country Hashed Potatoes and Cabbage ········· ¥3,900

テンダーロインステーキ カフェ・ド・パリ
Tournedos of Beef with Peppers, Onions and Cafe de Paris, Creamed Potatoes 100g ¥3,100
and Sauteed Cabbage 140g ¥3,900

フィレミニヨン ブラックペッパーソース
Fillet Mignon of Beef with Black Pepper Cognac Sauce, Creamed Potatoes with Crisp 100g ¥3,100
Onions, Sauteed Endives with Herbs 140g ¥3,900

ロースト プライムリブビーフ Lady's Cut(レディースカット) ¥6,500
Roasted Prime Rib of Beef, Gratined Potatoes, Vegetables King's Cut(キングカット) ¥7,500

51

restaurant
Grisanti's

location
Etobicoke, Ontario, Canada

design firm
Morris Graphics Ltd

art director
Michael Moran

designer/illustrator
Harvey Sedlack

year produced
1992

CONCEPT

Grisanti's menu's casual design appeals to
its broad-based market. The illustration of
a large, slightly off-balanced tomato and
pepper immediately relaxes guests. These
images continue throughout the menu, and
are used to promote certain special features
on the back page.

With each entrée category, a suggestion of a
wine is included for those customers who
may not be comfortable choosing a wine.

paper stock
12pt Cornwall C2S

number of color inks
Three

number produced
1,000

design budget
$6,000

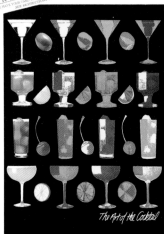

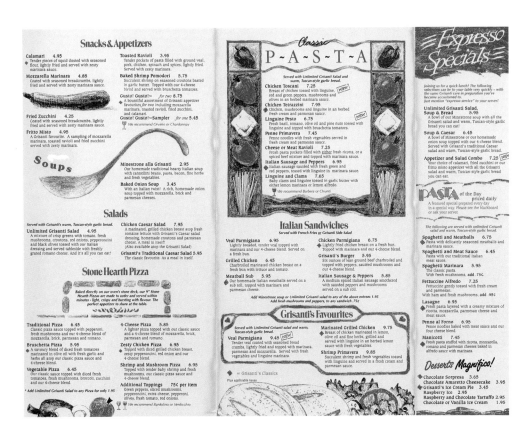

restaurant
Tucci Benucch

location
Seattle, Washington

design firm
Image Group Studios

designer/illustrator
George Toomer

photographer/copywriter
George Toomer

year produced
1993

CONCEPT

Tucci Benucch's interior design is based on an old Italian country home, each dining area representing an actual room. Tucci Benucch was originally a blending of authentic names, but to complete the reproduction theme, it became the first names of two sisters, each with identifiable personalities.

The menu looks like an old family scrapbook featuring photographs and memorabilia with vague captions, and supplies the story of the sisters and dates of activities to the reader. Hand lettering completes the effect. The menu is designed to be read in eight minutes...the standard set-up time.

SPECIAL VISUAL EFFECTS

The paper conveys the essence of old album paper when printed in two colors. To give a handwritten effect, each page was enhanced with tipped-in photographs of various sizes. The photos were printed on crack-n-peel adhesive stock with duotones and color tint blocks, as well as halftones, to give an old picture quality. They were then kiss-cut, to be easily applied later.

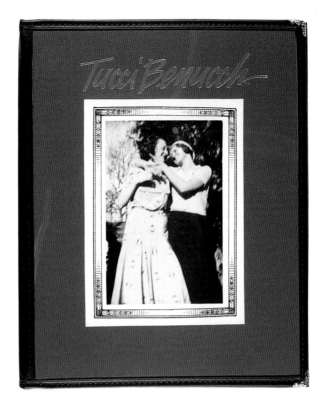

TRENDS FOR THE '90s

"...As competition grows, so too will the appeal of the individual restaurant...."

paper stock
80# Simpson Quest Cover Putty

typeface
Hand Lettering

printing technique
Offset Lithography 1250 Multilith on Inserts, 28" Harris Sheet-fed Photo Sheet

number produced
1,000

design budget
under $10,000

53

restaurant
Beaver Creek Tavern

location
Euro Disney, Paris, France

design firm
David Carter Design

designer
David Brashier

illustrator
Pat Foss *(Harter's engravings)*

year produced
1992

CONCEPT

Printed in English and French, menus for the Beaver Creek Tavern utilize old engravings of various fauna from the Rocky Mountains as illustrations. The menus are both light-weight and interchangeable.

SPECIAL VISUAL EFFECTS

The fibers in the French rayon paper stock create a very earthy and natural backdrop for the menu items.

paper stock
French Rayon

typefaces
Caslon, Optima

printing technique
Offset Lithography

number produced
1,000 of each *(three designs)*

EARLY MORNING STARTERS
Pour les matinaux

Mimosa 40F
Champagne orange

Champagne by the Glass 40F
Coupe de champagne

Bloody Mary 40F
*Vodka, jus de tomate, citron,
Worcestershire sauce, Tabasco*

FRESH FRUITS & JUICES
Fruits et jus de fruits frais

Fresh Squeezed Orange or Grapefruit Juice 20F
Orange ou pamplemousse pressé

Cranberry Juice, Apple Juice,
Tomato Juice, Prune Juice 15F
*Jus d'airelle, jus de pomme,
jus de tomate, jus de pruneaux*

Bowl of Fresh Seasonal Berries 35F
Coupe de fruits rouges de saison

Stewed Prunes 28F
Compote de pruneaux

Fresh Pink Grapefruit Segments 22F
Pamplemousse rose en quartiers

CEREALS
Céréales

Choice of Raisin Bran, Cornflakes,
All Bran or Rice Krispies 28F

With Berries or Sliced Bananas 38F
*Son nature, aux raisins secs, flocons
d'avoine ou riz croustillant*

Accompagnés de fruits rouges ou de bananes

Toasted Granola with
Yogurt and Honey 42F
*Craquelins d'avoine grillés accompagnés
de yaourt et de miel*

Hot Oatmeal with Raisins,
Cinnamon and Fresh Cream 35F
*Porridge aux raisins secs,
à la cannelle et à la crème*

BREAKFAST SPECIALS
Petits déjeuners du jour

TRAILFINDER'S CONTINENTAL 75F
Petit déjeuner du randonneur

Choice of Juice
Jus de fruits variés

Fresh Pink Grapefruit Segments
Pamplemousse rose en quartiers

Bakery Basket
Panier de petits pains

Coffee, Tea or Hot Chocolate
Café, thé ou chocolat chaud

MOUNTAIN FITNESS BREAKFAST 95F
Petit déjeuner allégé du montagnard

Choice of Juice
Jus de fruits variés

Fresh Seasonal Berries
Fruits rouges de saison

Toasted Granola with Yogurt and Honey
*Craquelins de flocons d'avoine grillés,
accompagnés de yaourt et de miel*

Coffee or Selection of Teas
Café ou sélection de thés

SEQUOIA SPECIAL 110F
La spécialité Sequoia

Choice of Juice
Jus de fruits variés

Two Eggs any Style
Deux oeufs à votre convenance

Smoked Bacon or Grilled Sausage
Bacon fumé ou saucisse grillée

Hash Brown Potatoes
Pommes de terre sautées

Bakery Basket
Panier de petits pains

Coffee, Tea or Hot Chocolate
Café, thé ou chocolat chaud

BEAVER CREEK SPECIALTIES
Les spécialités du Beaver Creek

Traditional Eggs Benedict 65F
*Oeufs Bénédicte
Deux oeufs pochés sur Muffin grillé avec
jambon canadien et sauce hollandaise*

Smoked Scottish Salmon, Cream
Cheese and Toasted Bagel 105F
*Saumon fumé d'Ecosse, fromage
frais et Bagel grillé*

Assorted Deli Meats and Sharp
Cheddar Cheese, a Boiled Egg to
Your Liking and Rolls 62F
*Assiette de charcuterie accompagnée de
cheddar, d'un oeuf à la coque comme vous
l'aimez et de petits pains*

Fresh Corned Beef Hash with a Poached Egg
Served on Toasted English Muffin 75F
*Corned beef maison et oeuf poché sur
Muffin grillé*

FRESH BAKED GOODS
Viennoiserie

Hard Roll 8F
Petit pain

Croissant 12F
Croissant

Blueberry Muffin 15F
Muffin aux myrtilles

Raisin Bran Muffin 15F
Muffin au son et raisins secs

Toasted English Muffin 12F
English Muffin grillé

BEVERAGES
Boissons

Fresh Brewed Coffee, Decaffeinated
Coffee, Select Teas or Milk 12F
Café, café décaféiné, sélection de thés ou lait

Hot Chocolate 12F
Chocolat chaud

Net Prices ✳ Prix Nets
Pipe and Cigar Smoking is Accepted in the Bar Only ✳ Cigares et pipes sont permis dans le Bar seulement

restaurant
Spasso Restaurant *(Grand Hyatt, Erawan Bangkok)*

location
Bangkok, Thailand

design firm
David Carter Design

designers
Kevin Prejean
Brian Moss

illustrator
Kevin Prejean

year produced
1992

CONCEPT
Spasso means 'fun' and 'amusement' in Italian. The shapes in the logo and layout convey the definition.

paper stock
Centura Gloss

typeface
Futura Condensed

printing technique
Offset Lithography

number of color inks
Three

number produced
250

restaurant
La Cazuela

location
Northampton, Massachusetts

designer
Barry Steeves

CONCEPT

A selection of warm, Southwestern colors
and graphic elements give La Cazuela's
menus a novel yet cohesive look. The
menus are hand-cut and pasted together,
making no two menus alike. La Cazuela
means "earthen cooking pot." Therefore,
the only constant graphic that ties the
menus together is the image of the
steaming pot.

To allow for greater flexibility, the inside
sheets are printed on a Macintosh computer and photocopied. A plastic menu jacket
holds the whole package together.

paper stock
Beckett Desert Haze *(inside)*
Mixed Color Stock *(covers)*

typeface
Univers 55

printing technique
Photocopy

number produced
40

design budget
$600-700 *(materials)*

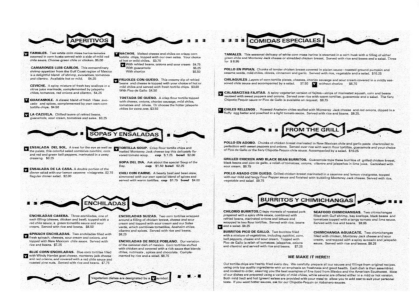

AUNT CHILADA'S

restaurant
Aunt Chilada's (*Pointe Hilton Resort, Squaw Peak*)

location
Phoenix, Arizona

design firm
DRi Communications

art director/designer
Dana Shetter

illustrator
Jeff Jones

copywriter
Paul Morris

year produced
1993

CONCEPT

Aunt Chilada's menu matches their festive "fiesta" atmosphere and Mexican-themed decor, with a Mexican flavor and Southwest feeling. The borders, inspired by the use of intricate borders in traditional Mexican artwork, have a rough textural look, while the edges are softened. The earth tones are reminiscent of the Sonoran Desert landscape around Phoenix. The illustration on the cover is a variation of the restaurant's old logo, while other symbols reflect the images of old Mexico.

SPECIAL VISUAL EFFECTS

The project was done entirely by hand. The borders are transfers in PMS colors and the images are cutouts of colored paper. The black was illustrated separately and converted into film positive.

TRENDS FOR THE '90s

"I'm a big fan of dining out with friends and family and expect to be seeing more menus using recycled papers and soybean-based inks reflecting healthier food selections."

paper stock
80# Productolith Gloss Cover

typefaces
Sarah Elizabeth (*headlines*)
Trajanus (*body copy*)

printing technique
Offset Lithography

number of color inks
Six

number produced
1,000

design budget
$4,000

Blast from the Past

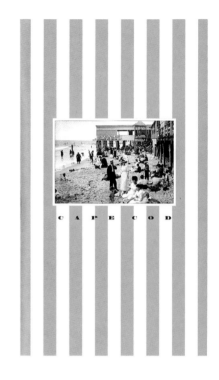

restaurant
Cape Cod Restaurant *(Newport Bay Club)*

location
Euro Disney, Paris, France

design firm
David Carter Design

designer
Lori Wilson

photographer
archive photography

year produced
1992

CONCEPT

Through the use of the cover photographs and colorful stripes, Cape Cod Restaurant's menu brings back the "boardwalk" days of the East Coast beach resorts.

paper stock
Starwhite

typeface
Bodoni Bold

printing technique
Offset Lithography

number of color inks
Four

number produced
500

restaurant
Club Manhattan *(Hotel New York)*

location
Euro Disney, Paris, France

design firm
David Carter Design

designer
Sharon LeJeune

illustrator
Margaret Kasahara

year produced
1992

CONCEPT

These elegant menus coordinate with the
elegant and sophisticated 1930s New York
theme of the hotel.

paper stock
Varied

typefaces
Stuyvesant, Parisian

printing technique
Offset Lithography

number of color inks
Four Metallic Inks, Black (x2)

number produced
2,500

ALAN COOK

restaurant
The Great Lost Bear

location
Portland, Maine

art director/designer
Weslie Evans

illustrators
Weslie Evans
Joe Muir

photographer
Randal Powers *(photo artist)*

copywriters
Weslie Evans
Dave Evans
Doug MacConnell

year produced
1991

CONCEPT

The menu design was inspired by a collection of tacky postcards and the motto, "support your right to arm bears." The road sign that appears on the menu is a local Maine landmark with a temporary "Great Lost Bear" sign attached.

SPECIAL VISUAL EFFECTS

The cover image is made up of three separate photographs. A sepia-tone print was hand-colored using bright colors to duplicate the aged look of an old postcard.

paper stock
Coated Recycled Paper

typeface
Hand Lettered *(by Weslie Evans)*

printing technique
Offset Lithography

number of color inks
Four

number produced
5,000

design budget
$300

THE
GREAT LOST BEAR

SALUTES THE
BANANA REPUBLICS

TROPICAL COCKTAILS
ISLAND BEERS
CARIBBEAN SPECIALS
HOT FUN &
FREE BANANAS!

MEXICALI MADNESS! '89
DAILY SOUTHWESTERN
SPECIALS
THE MEXICALI BLUES
FEATURING:
MINI BLUE NACHOS 2.00
&
BLUE MARGARITA JELLO
FROM HELL 2.00
MEXICAN BEER SPECIALS
MEXICALI MADNESS T-SHIRT
10.00

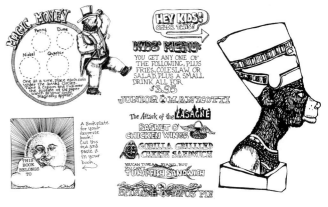

63

restaurant
801 Steak & Chop House

location
Des Moines, Iowa

design firm
Sayles Graphic Design

designer/illustrator
John Sayles

photographs
archival

copywriters
Wendy Lyons
Terri Wolf

year produced
1993

CONCEPT

The design of the graphics was developed to reflect the feel of a 1920s steak house with an updated flair. Print collateral is beautifully orchestrated with attention to various details. Environmental graphics also tie in to this "master plan."

TRENDS FOR THE '90s

"The main trend will be a shift away from 'traditional' formats. More than ever, restaurant owners will realize that menu design is a significant part of a restaurant's image. There also seems to be an increasing concern among owners about ecology issues. We see fewer laminated menus...and an increased use of recycled paper stocks."

paper stock
James River Terra

typefaces
Hand Lettering, Futura, Galliard

printing technique
Offset Lithography

number of color inks
Three

number produced
500

BILL NELLANS

BILL NELLANS

BILL NELLAN

64

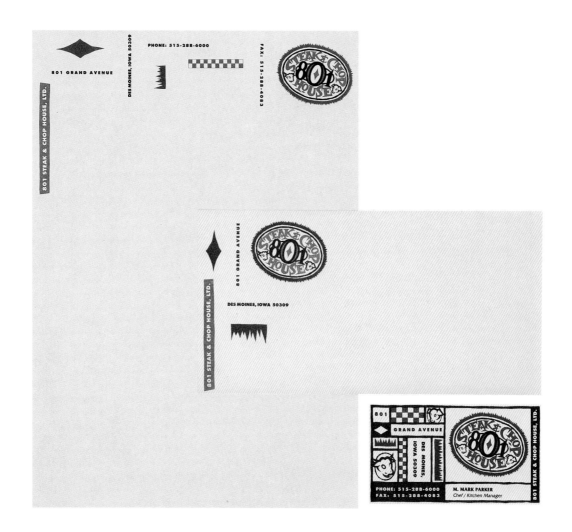

BILL NELLANS

BILL NELLANS

65

restaurant
Sweetriver Saloon

location
Merced, California

design firm
Belyea Design

designer
Patricia Belyea

illustrator
Richard Kehl

copywriter
Celeste Souza

year produced
1993

CONCEPT

The restaurant's walls are laden with memorabilia, and the menu continues this theme. The menu masters are painted in collage with a green background. Future versions will be imprinted in two colors.

TRENDS FOR THE '90s

"Menus that can be changed easily—sometimes daily. Well-designed laser printers for laser-printed pieces will be common."

paper stock
Kimdura

typefaces
Copperplate, Brush Script

printing technique
Waterless Lithography

number of color inks
Five, Two

number produced
200 Imprints
12,000 Masters

design budget
$6,000

restaurant
Wooly Bully's *(Northville)*

location
Northville, Michigan

design firm
Crown Printing

designer
Dennis Cassidy

illustrator
Chris Franchi

copywriter
Mark Roman

year produced
1993

CONCEPT

The design approach captures a '50s hard-rock, rock n' roll feeling through the use of guitars and memorabilia, like posters of Elvis, mounted on the walls. A 1957 pink Cadillac juts through the wall on one side of the building, while a 1964 Corvette hangs in the entryway. A Wooly Wear shop sells shirts, hats, shorts and other souvenir items.

SPECIAL VISUAL EFFECTS

The back cover of the menu has stylized photos of Elvis, substituting the head of Wooly Man.

TRENDS FOR THE '90s

"There seems to be a current trend for the less expensive approach of plastic jackets and computer printed sheets. However, I find the serious, well-conceived establishment still requires a well thought of, attractive, well-organized format that will complement his decor and theme featuring menu items that he wishes to sell. This is done by the use of photography."

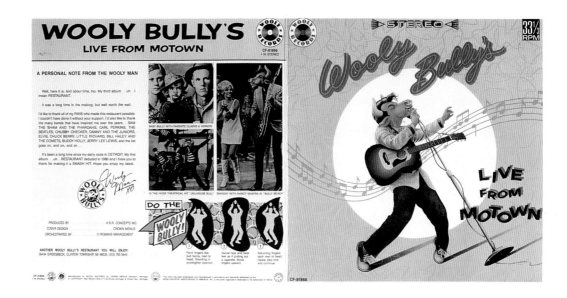

paper stock
12pt Productolith

typefaces
Kabel Medium, Demi, Bold

printing technique
Offset Lithography

number of color inks
Four-color Process
PMS on Insert and Inside Cover

number produced
2,000

design budget
$10,000

restaurant
Wooly Bully's *(Mt. Clemens)*

location
Mt. Clemens, Michigan

design firm
Crown Printing

designer/illustrator
Dan Nolin

copywriter
Mark Roman

year produced
1991

CONCEPT

The 1950s diner style is apparent in this restaurant as the front of the building is constructed to look like a jukebox, and a large 45" record comprises the dance floor. A 1957 Chevy is cut out for the disk jockey.

The menu is loaded with different images that call the '50s to mind, including Superman, a roller-skating waitress and a jukebox which features "Tutti Frutti," "Hound Dog," and of course, "Wooly Bully."

TRENDS FOR THE '90s

"A design that will last a longer period of time without becoming stale, not trendy, yet allowing quick, economical changes in items and prices."

paper stock
12pt Productolith

typefaces
Antique Olive CD *(insert)*

printing technique
Die-cut and Lamination

number of color inks
Four

number produced
2,000

design budget
$10,000

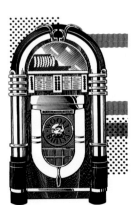

restaurant
Rock-Ola Cafe

location
Greensboro, North Carolina

design firm
Kenyon Press

designer/illustrator
Dick Witt

photographs
supplied

year produced
1993

CONCEPT

The Rock-Ola chain of restaurants has a strong rock n' roll theme and a fun, upbeat atmosphere. The menu design features illustrations of rock n' roll memorabilia from the 1950s to the 1990s. Some of the illustrations are based on actual artifacts on display as interior design elements. Brightly colored copy blocks and creative headings add to the friendly, party atmosphere.

paper stock
10pt Carolina C2S

typeface
Kabel

printing technique
Offset Lithography

number of color inks
Four-color Process

number produced
31,000

restaurant
Dalt's

location
Dallas, Texas

design firm
Stafford Ream, Inc.

designer
Ed Stafford

photographer
Ka Chen Yeung

year produced
1993

CONCEPT

A sepia-toned photographic collage depicting images and small antique mementos of the 1940s captures the nostalgic feeling of this '40s diner.

paper stock
100# Warren LOE Dull Cream Cover

typeface
Novarese

printing technique
Offset Lithography

number of color inks
Four-color Process, Two-color Imprint

number produced
1,000

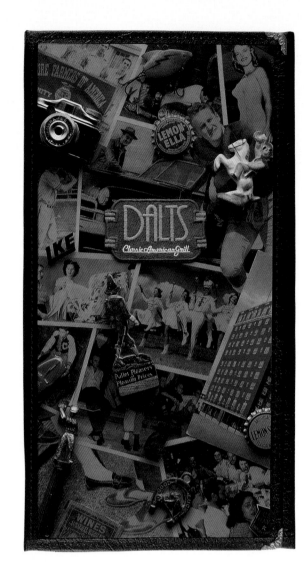

PLATE DINNERS

A House Salad or Caesar Dinner Salad may be added for an additional $1.45

Charbroiled Breast of Chicken	$6.95	**Angel Hair Pasta with Shrimp**	$8.25
Served on a bed of rice with steamed fresh vegetables and your choice of one side item		Angel hair pasta with sautéed shrimp, tomatoes and basil tossed in a light, white wine sauce	
✓ **Chicken Fingers**	$6.95	**Linguini Stir Fry**	$6.95
Served with Hand-Cut Fries, barbecue or honey mustard sauce for dipping and your choice of one side item		A spicy stir fried blend of chicken and fresh cut vegetables. Tossed with linguini in a teriyaki sauce	
✓ **Chicken Puff Pie**	$5.45		
A flaky pastry shell stuffed with tender chicken and vegetables		✓ **Fish and Chips**	$5.75
		Cold-water fillets lightly battered and deep-fried golden brown. Served with Hand-Cut Fries and your choice of one side item	
Southwest Quesadillas	$5.95		
A grilled flour tortilla filled with sliced beef or chicken, jalapeño, onions, tomatoes, green peppers and cheese		**Fish of the Day**	
		Ask your server about today's fish selection. Served with your choice of one side item	
Dalts Taquitos	$5.95		
Chicken, cheese, green onions and jalapeños rolled in crisp corn tortillas. Served with salsa, guacamole and sour cream		**Baby Back Ribs & Chicken Combo**	$10.95
		A half-slab of Dalts Baby Back Ribs with a barbecue breast of chicken. Served with Hand-Cut Fries and your choice of one side item	
Strip Steak Dinner	$11.95		
A 12 oz. U.S.D.A. Choice New York strip steak seasoned and charbroiled to perfection. Served with a loaded baked potato and your choice of one side item		✓ **Baby Back Ribs**	
		Dalts famous tender ribs, marinated and charbroiled. Served with Hand-Cut Fries and your choice of one side item	
Smothered Steak	$7.95	Half Slab	$6.95
U.S.D.A. choice sirloin topped with sautéed mushrooms, onions and melted Provolone cheese. Served with a loaded baked potato and your choice of one side item		Full Slab	$10.95
		Fajitas	
		Choice of charbroiled steak, chicken or a combination	
		For One	$7.25
		For Two	$13.45

BLUEPLATE SPECIALS

Sunday/Monday Meatloaf	**Thursday** Shrimp Special
Tuesday Pot Roast	**Friday/Saturday** Prime Rib
Wednesday Manager's Special	

SIDES		
Steamed Vegetables	Ranch Beans	Rice
Mashed Potatoes	Cinnamon Apples	Pasta Pilaf
	Macaroni & Cheese	

© Dalts DАTT 1985. MKATE R

APPETIZERS

Fried Provolone	$3.75	Loaded Potato Skins	$4.95
✓ Chargrilled Wings	$5.95	Thin Onion Rings	$2.95
Buffalo Wings	$5.95	Hand Cut Cheese Fries	$2.95
Spinach Con Queso	$5.95	Loaded Hand Cut Fries	$3.95
✓ Spinach Artichoke Dip	$4.75	Chicken Fingers	$4.95

SOUPS & SALADS

✓ **Baked Potato Soup**		✓ **Chicken Fajita Caesar**	$6.25
Cup	$1.95	Sizzling strips of charbroiled chicken breast served on top of our Southwestern-style Caesar salad	
Bowl	$2.75		
Soup of the Day			
Cup	$1.95	**Caesar Salad**	$3.95
Bowl	$2.75	**House Salad**	$2.75
French Onion Soup		Mixed greens with tomatoes and carrots, topped with eggs and cheese	
Bowl	$3.50		
		✓ **Chicken Stir Fry**	$6.25
		Marinated chicken breast and fresh vegetables stir-fried in a spicy teriyaki dressing and served over mixed greens. Topped with Jack cheese	
		Southwestern Salad	$6.45
		Charbroiled chicken! Mixed greens, tomatoes, black olives, avocado and cheeses	

BURGERS & SANDWICHES

Gardenburger	$4.95	**Philadelphia Cheese Steak**	$6.25
A wholesome burger of nuts, mushrooms and whole grains served classic style. Accompanied with Dalts Pasta Pilaf		Thinly sliced U.S.D.A. Choice sirloin steak, smothered in Provolone cheese, green peppers and grilled onions. Served with Hand-Cut Fries	
Turkey Burger	$4.95		
100% white meat turkey patty served traditional burger-style. Accompanied with Dalts Pasta Pilaf		✓ **Monterey Club**	$6.25
		A Southwestern Club with marinated chicken, ham, bacon, cheese and mild jalapeños stacked three high on whole wheat flour tortillas. Served with Hand-Cut Fries	
American Cheeseburger	$5.45		
Served with Hand-Cut Fries and Ranch Beans		**Hamburger Club**	$6.65
American Bacon Cheeseburger	$5.75	Dalts cheeseburger with bacon, lettuce and tomatoes on whole wheat toast with mayonnaise and Thousand Island dressing. Served with Hand-Cut Fries	
Served with Hand-Cut Fries and Ranch Beans			
✓ **San Francisco Dinner Club**	$6.95		
Charbroiled breast of chicken, bacon, tomatoes and lettuce on grilled, authentic San Francisco sourdough with Swiss cheese, mayonnaise and honey mustard. Served with Hand-Cut Fries			

At Dalts, our fries are hard-cut from premium Idaho potatoes, then cooked using our special double frying procedure to bring you the best French fries possible.

MALTS & DRINKS

Huge Iced Tea or Fountain Soft Drinks	$1.25	✓ **Old Fashioned Milkshakes and Malts**	$2.75
Free refills		Vanilla, chocolate, strawberry, mocha or cherry	
Perrier			
Fresh Ground Coffee	$1.00	**Ice Cream Sodas and Floats**	$2.25
Decaffeinated Coffee or Hot Tea	$1.00		

✓ marks our "Specialty" items   © Dalts DATT 1985. MKATE R

DESSERTS

✓ **Cinnamon Apple Puff**	$2.75	**Mocha Almond Fudge Pie**	$3.95
A flaky pastry shell loaded with cinnamon apples and topped with a scoop of vanilla ice cream.		Chocolate and mocha ice cream covered with chocolate cookies and hot fudge	
Dalts Classic Chocolate Malt Cake	$2.75	**Pie of the Day**	
A la mode, 65¢		Ask your server about today's featured cream pies or Dalts fresh baked fruit pies	
Ice Cream Sundae	$2.65	✓ **Dalts Drizzle Cake**	$2.25
Hot fudge, hot caramel, chocolate or strawberry		A chocolate mocha concoction topped with vanilla ice cream.	
Key Lime Pie	$2.45		

✓ marks our "Specialty" items   © Dalts DATT 1985. MKATE R

restaurant
Rio Ranch House

location
Houston, Texas

design firm
Express Foods

designer
Lonnie Schiller

illustrators
Lisa Del Grande
Joe Heins

copywriters
Robert Del Grande
Lonnie Schiller *(menus)*
Lisa Del Grande *(key cards)*

year produced
1993

CONCEPT

The concept for the menu design comes directly from the central theme of Rio Ranch. The restaurant is styled after the early 1900s working ranch houses of West Texas—limestone walls, cedar trees for supporting posts, wood beams, a grand stone fireplace in the main dining room and a collection of cowboy art and Western antiques. The children's Buckaroo Games menu is loaded with activities to keep young diners occupied.

SPECIAL VISUAL EFFECTS

Visual effects are fairly simple yet very textural in design and give the effect of fun in an updated historical manner.

Stuart Roy
Manager

RIO RANCH
T E X A S

9999 Westheimer
Houston, Texas 77042
(713) 952-5000
Fax (713) 952-2263

RANCH HOUSE MEALS

Served Ranch House Style with:
Mixed Lettuce Salad with Croutons
Basket of Muffins, Biscuits & Corn Bread
Baked Potato with Bacon, Cheese, Sour Cream & Chives
Ranch Style Red Beans
Green Beans

Crispy Fried Wrangler Specialities

Butterflied Deep Fried Shrimp	$11.95
Chicken Fried Sirloin Steak *with Black Peppercorn Cream Gravy*	$9.95
Buttermilk Fried Chicken	$9.95
Fried Chicken "Spicy Wings Style"	$9.95
Corn Meal Fried Quail	$12.50

Cowboy Favorites from the Wood Burning Grill
with our selection of sauces

Grilled Shrimp with Bacon, Mushrooms, Onions & Jalapeno	$12.50
Fresh Fish of the Day	$12.50
Half Chicken Slow Roasted with BBQ Rub	$9.95
Breast of Chicken with Green Chiles & Cheese	$10.95
Slow Grilled Duckling with Tabasco & Molasses	$12.95
Broken Arrow Ranch Venison Sausage	$11.95
Chile Marinated 10 oz Sirloin Steak	$11.95
Aged 12 oz New York Strip Steak	$15.50
Aged 12 oz Ribeye Steak	$14.95
Aged 10 oz Fillet of Beef	$15.95
16 oz T-Bone Steak	$18.95

DESSERTS

Pecan Pie $2.50
Ice Cream Sundae with Pecans & Rich Chocolate Sauce $3.50
Blueberry Cobbler with Vanilla Ice Cream $3.25
Vanilla Ice Cream $1.00

"Where the West Shines ...on real good times"

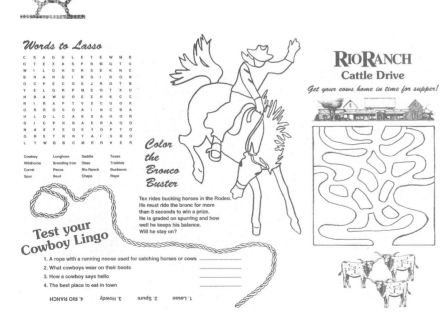

Words to Lasso

C	S	A	D	D	L	E	T	E	W	M	B
O	T	E	X	A	S	P	B	M	Q	T	U
W	I	L	D	H	O	R	S	E	K	N	C
B	R	A	N	D	I	N	G	I	R	O	N
O	C	P	E	C	O	S	J	R	O	T	B
Y	E	L	G	R	P	M	E	O	T	X	U
N	D	A	W	U	O	E	E	H	K	C	C
R	I	R	A	P	T	V	X	C	U	O	K
O	R	R	O	S	G	A	I	N	C	B	A
G	I	C	P	N	B	A	E	R	A	O	R
N	A	X	Y	E	O	E	Y	O	P	T	O
O	R	E	T	R	R	T	A	I	S	R	O
L	T	W	Q	B	C	M	R	R	V	E	R

Cowboy · Longhorn · Saddle · Texas
Wildhorse · Branding Iron · Steer · Trailride
Corral · Pecos · Rio Ranch · Buckaroo
Spur · Boot · Chaps · Rope

Color the Bronco Buster

Tex rides bucking horses in the Rodeo. He must ride the bronc for more than 8 seconds to win a prize. He is graded on spurring and how well he keeps his balance. Will he stay on?

Test your Cowboy Lingo

1. A rope with a running noose used for catching horses or cows _____
2. What cowboys wear on their boots
3. How a cowboy says hello
4. The best place to eat in town

4. RIO RANCH   3. Howdy   2. Spurs   1. Lasso

RIO RANCH
Cattle Drive
Get your cows home in time for supper!

TRENDS FOR THE '90s

"Two significant trends in menu design are flexibility and cost-effectiveness. The '90s restaurant must never become stagnant in its food presentation. Therefore, a menu design that will easily accommodate a major change inexpensively is most important."

paper stock
60# Hammermill Cream

typefaces
Hanna Graphics

printing technique
New Ink
Offset Lithography

number of color inks
Four, Dull Varnish

number produced
2,500

design budget
$10,000

restaurant
The Bella Union

location
Tombstone, Arizona

design firm
David Sanford & Jim Spencer

designers/illustrators
David Sanford
Jim Spencer

year produced
1991

CONCEPT

The design of The Bella Union's menus was conceived with Tombstone's 1880s prime time in mind. Although most think of Tombstone as the "Wild West," the design instead conveys the other side of the coin, showing the social life and pleasant activities of the 1880s in both the new menu and the restaurant ambiance and restoration.

SPECIAL VISUAL EFFECTS

The menu reflects the only true medium that was available to the early Western pioneers, the newspaper. Customers enjoy reading the authentic history of our world-famous Western town while waiting to be seated, or for their meals to arrive. Most buy them for souvenirs.

TRENDS FOR THE '90s

"Co-operative advertising. Our next issue will have ad space for sale to other businesses in town. Not only will we get free menus, but the menu will actually make a profit."

paper stock
Newsprint (50% recycled)

typefaces
P.T. Barnum, Roman, Gothic

printing technique
Desktop, Newsprint

number of color inks
One

number produced
30,000

design budget
$500 (including printing)

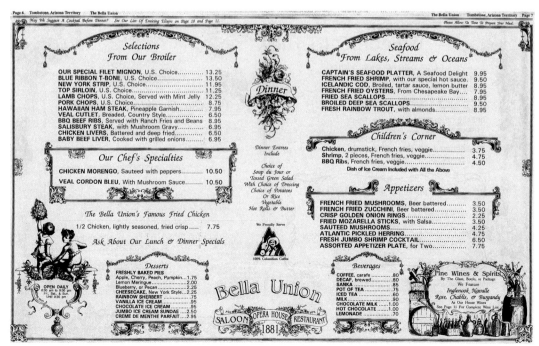

restaurant
Parkside Diner *(Hotel New York)*

location
Euro Disney, Paris, France

design firm
David Carter Design

designer
Sharon LeJeune

photographer
FPG *(archive stock)*

copywriter
Marsha Coburn

year produced
1992

CONCEPT

The Hotel New York has a 1930s theme and was designed to be reminiscent of New York's Rainbow Room. Updated inserts are easily replaced.

paper stock
Warren LOE Dull

typefaces
Parisian, Kabel

printing technique
Offset Lithography

number of color inks
Three PMS, Varnish

number produced
1,500

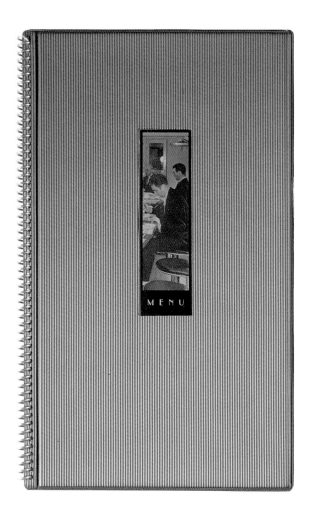

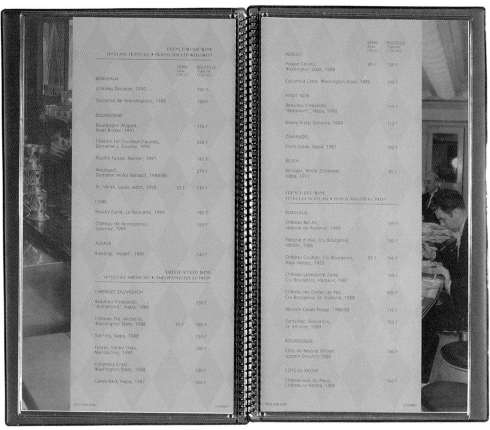

restaurant
McGinnis Landing Restaurant

location
London, Ontario, Canada

design firm
Falco Design Inc.

designer
Grace Falco

photographer
Bob Chambers Photography

copywriters
Bob DiFruscia
Grace Falco

year produced
1992

CONCEPT

To emphasize the quality and atmosphere of McGinnis Landing Restaurant, the menu was designed to be easy-to-read and totally functional. The menu is also flexible in its ability to have copy imprints changed on individual pages.

SPECIAL VISUAL EFFECTS

Menu photographs include a curio box and various antiques. A 40-year-old refrigerator and an eclectic array of magnets give McGinnis Landing's menu its homey appeal. The menu cover is a photograph of the curio box stuffed with objects related to food or the restaurant's memorabilia-cluttered interiors. Inside the menu, items are presented as notes stuck on the refrigerator by magnets.

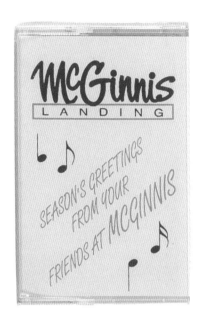

TRENDS FOR THE '90s

"Functional, cost-effective, entertaining."

paper stock
10pt Cornwall

typeface
Italia *(Book & Medium)*

printing technique
Offset Lithography *(200-Line Screen)*

number of color inks
Four-color Process

number produced
10,000

design budget
$4,500

restaurant
Park Avenue Cafe

location
New York, New York

design firm
Monica Banks and Company

designer/illustrator
Monica Banks

copywriter
Kevin Dillon

year produced
1992

CONCEPT

Built around an early American woodcut of a sheaf of wheat, Park Avenue Cafe's logo makes the restaurant seem as if it's been around for a long time. Wheat is also a big theme in the interior of the restaurant.

SPECIAL VISUAL EFFECTS

The menus look like photo albums. Fifteen different historical photos are used which refer to themes in the restaurant: wheat, cooking, American flags, historical pictures of New York.

TRENDS FOR THE '90s

"All of this in-house word processing creates a new challenge for the graphic designer, calling for new resourcefulness and ingenuity in design. The designer must find other tools to create images to define the character of a restaurant...."

paper stock
90# Cordivan Cover

typeface
Caslon

printing technique
Offset Lithography

number produced
500

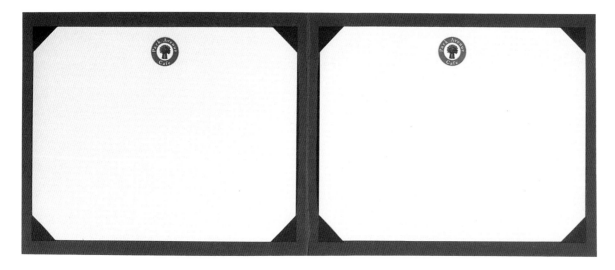

restaurant
Counter Culture

location
San Francisco, California

design firm
Desktop By Design

designer/illustrator
Chris de Heer

copywriter
Cathy de Heer

year produced
1992

CONCEPT

The interior architecture at Counter Culture is that of a European-style food boutique, but the restaurant is primarily a catering and take-out restaurant. The logo has a sort of '60s cartoon feel to it. The menu conveys a combination of '60s cartoon angles with the traditional feel of the interior. The large amount of copy underscores the need for a typographic approach. One color emphasizes the typographic and graphic simplicity.

SPECIAL VISUAL EFFECTS

The starburst effect meets the mood requirements without overwhelming the typography. It also allows a variety of screen tints to be introduced, adding some richness to the cover. The starbursts on the front and back cover were created in Adobe Illustrator with extensive use of the mask feature.

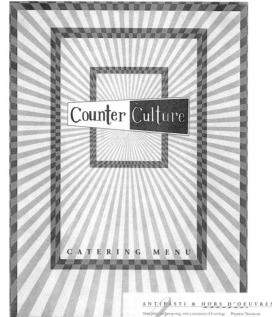

TRENDS FOR THE '90s

"...the availability of hundreds of typefaces and the maturation of the computer-literate design community are leading to a reinterpretation of old styles and a renewed appreciation for typography. Menus in particular will benefit from this retrospective because restaurants, more than many businesses, rely on image...."

paper stock
Simpson

typefaces
Adobe Garamond, Kuenstler

printing technique
Offset Lithography

number of color inks
One

number produced
2,000

design budget
Trade Agreement

77

restaurant
Marlene *(Hotel Inter•Continental Berlin)*

location
Berlin, Germany

design firm
David Carter Design

designer
David Brashier

illustrator
Michael Crampton

year produced
1993

CONCEPT

Marlene's Lounge is themed around the persona of actress Marlene Dietrech. Throughout the menu, brushed illustrations depict Marlene over the various stages of her career, and the typography, borders and even the menu items themselves are reflective of her era.

paper stock
Trophy Gloss Cover

typefaces
Broadway, Futura

printing technique
Offset Lithography

number of color inks
Four *(on each side)*

number produced
1,000

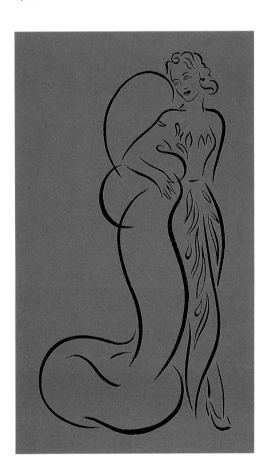

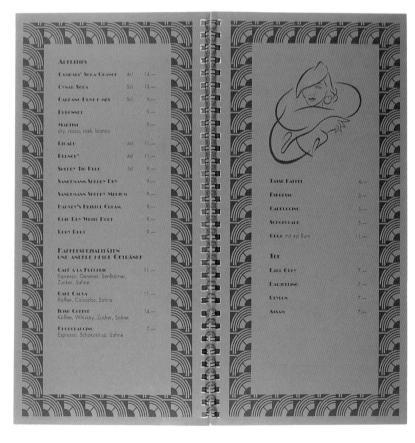

restaurant
The Mity Nice Grill

location
Chicago, Illinois

design firm
True Ideas

designer
Cynthia Kerby

illustrator
Mity Nice Grill

copywriter
Kevin J. Brown

year produced
1993

CONCEPT

The Mity Nice Grill is a 1940s grill with updated ideas on an older concept recapturing a simpler time when people were just plain nice to one another. The atmosphere is warm and comfortable, and the restaurant is very family-friendly.

SPECIAL VISUAL EFFECTS

The design of the restaurant gives it an inviting look with a wide range of appeal. Three-foot pictures of smiling children adorn the walls, enhancing the feeling of being "mity welcome."

paper stock
80# Fox River Confetti *(color: Ninja)*

typefaces
Futura Heavy & Medium
Coronet Bold, Kaufmann Bold

printing technique
Offset Lithography

number of color inks
One

number produced
1,000

design budget
$5,000

restaurant
Peninsula Fountain & Grill

location
Palo Alto, California

design firm
THARP DID IT

designers
Rick Tharp
Jana Heer

illustrator
Jana Heer

copywriter
Rob Fischer

year produced
1990

CONCEPT

The graphics program "utilizes both '20s vernacular and Neanderthal technique." According to designer Rick Tharp, "It was important to the owner that we not 'overdesign' any of the menus, signage or graphics. He wanted it to look as though a designer was not involved in the process." An element of humor is present in the overall design. The clock shown on the opposite page reads "EAT AND GET OUT (just kidding!)."

The design has retained the integrity of the original logotype, giving personality to the soda jerk that has been used for the past 70 years.

TRENDS FOR THE '90s

"I do not have my finger on the pulse of restaurant design. We just do what's right. This identity won't win any design awards, but it was the right solution for the place."

DESIGN: THARP DID IT ON RECYCLED PAPER

LAURIE FISCHER
Licensed Fountaineer

566 Emerson Street
Palo Alto, CA 94301
Phone 415.323.3131
No Fax Machine. Yet!

SINCE P 1923

Welcome to the Peninsula Fountain & Grille. In 1923 the Peninsula Dairy opened this place and through the years it has managed to survive. Although the faces of our servers have changed, the original concept remains the same. Great Food . . . Great Shakes . . . Reasonable Prices. We know you all miss the grumpy old waitresses who used to bicker all day long. Somehow we just know this place never would have made it without them.

There are a few things we would like to set the record straight on. Please don't ask us how the old girls are, you know the ones, because we don't know. And about those 15¢ shakes: Get real! And, yes, the Peninsula Creamery still makes ice cream three blocks from here. Chances are we don't remember, "way back when", you first started coming here, but we're glad to see some things never change.

The bathrooms are still upstairs and, no, we don't have a pay phone, never mind a FAX. About the music, well, the records are so old they all play at different volumes, sometimes loud, sometimes not so loud. Oh well, as we say at the counter, that's life. Maybe we don't do everything the way you like, but we'll do our best. If that's not good enough make us an offer we can't refuse!

We love to see all of you but, you could come in a little more often.

Thanks for spending all your
time and money with us!

Rob & Laurie

P.S. If you're not from Palo Alto this probably won't make any sense.

BEVERAGES

Fresh Squeezed Juices:
Orange 1.50/1.95
Grapefruit 1.50/1.95
Apple Juice 1.00
Pineapple Juice 1.00
Tomato Juice 1.00
V-8 Juice 1.00
Lemonade 1.10
Milk 1.10
Hot Chocolate 1.10
Coffee & Tea .... .80
Iced Tea 1.10
Yoo Hoo 1.00

Coke 1.10
Cherry Coke 1.25
Vanilla Coke 1.25
Root Beer 1.10
Sprite 1.10
Green River 1.25
Soux City Cream Soda.. 1.25
Mineral Water 1.00
Kentucky NIP 1.25
IBC Root Beer 1.25
IBC Birch Beer 1.25
IBC Sasparilla 1.25
Dr. Brown's 1.00

BREAKFUST

Fresh Fruit Bowl 3.25
Homemade Granola 2.25
Cereal (hot or cold, served with milk) 1.75
    with fruit 2.95
Yogurt, Fruit and Granola Parfait 3.95
Pancakes 3.75
Belgian Waffle 3.95
    With Fruit 5.25
French Toast 3.75
Eggs with Bacon, Ham or Sausage 5.25
Two Eggs (any style) 3.25
Three Egg Omelette or Scramble
    with your choice of three items 5.50

Ham • Mushrooms • Bacon • Green Chilies • Cream Cheese
Tomatoes • Green Onion • Avocado • Sour Cream • Spinach
Cheddar Cheese • Swiss Cheese • American Cheese • Jack Cheese

Extra items add .75 each

HOUSE SPECIALS

NY Steak and Eggs 7.50
Cajun Scramble 5.75
Hash Brown Pie with
    Two Eggs (any style).. 5.50

Potato Pancakes 5.95
Banana Pecan
    Waffle 4.95
Spinach, Mushroom, Cream
    Cheese Scramble 5.50

All of the above egg dishes served with hash browns or home fries,
buttered toast & jelly. English muffin or bagel substitution, add .20.

SIDE ORDERS

Home Fries 1.50
Hash Brown Potatoes ... 1.50
One Egg 1.10
Cinnamon Toast 1.00
English Muffin 1.00
Country Sausage (3) ... 2.75
Cajun Sausage 2.75

Ham 2.50
Bacon (4) 2.50
Buttered Toast .... .80
Bagel 1.00
    with Cream Cheese .. 1.50
Homemade Muffin 1.25
Homemade Coffee Cake 1.50

SALADS

Served with your choice of Ranch, Thousand Island, Blue Cheese or
Italian Dressing

Tuna Salad 5.95
Fresh Fruit Plate 5.95
    w/ Cottage Cheese .. 6.95
Southern Fried Chicken
    Salad 6.95

Chicken Salad 5.95
Cobb Salad 6.95
Chinese Chicken
    Salad 6.95
Spinach Salad 6.95

SANDWICHES

All sandwiches served with your choice of potato salad or coleslaw
and pickle chips

Fried Egg & Bacon 4.25
Hot Dog 3.25
Chili Dog 4.25
French Dip 4.50
Egg & Olive 3.95
Turkey Club 6.25
BLT 4.25
Egg Salad 3.75
Roast Beef 4.25
Turkey Breast 4.50
Grilled Chicken 5.75
Soup & 1/2 Sandwich .. 4.25

Hot Pastrami 4.75
Reuben 4.95
NY Steak Sandwich ... 7.25
Grilled Cheese, Bacon
    & Tomato 4.75
Grilled Ham & Cheese . 4.75
Tuna 4.25
Chicken Salad 4.25
Grilled Cheese 3.50
Philly Cheese Steak .. 5.75
Tuna Melt 4.75
Chicken Salad Melt ... 4.75

Grilled Meatloaf Sandwich 5.25

HAMBURGERS

All of our burgers are made with 1/2 lb. of freshly ground beef
and served with grilled onions and pickle chips

Hamburger 3.60
Cheeseburger 3.95
California Burger 5.35
Swiss & Mushroom
    Burger 4.85
Ortega Burger 4.50

Patty Melt with Grilled
    Onions 4.25
Chili Burger 4.75
BBQ Bacon Burger 4.50
Velveeta Burger 3.95
Swiss & Bacon Burger . 5.15

With French Fries add .75   With Bacon add .75

KEEP GOING

it's a
knockout!

THE PENINSULA
MILKSHAKE—
in 7 delicious flavors
CHOCOLATE
ROCKY ROAD
STRAWBERRY
MARSHMALLOW
BUTTERSCOTCH
MAPLE
VANILLA MALT

Peninsula Creamery

566
EMERSON
HAMILTON

paper stock
Simpson Evergreen Recycled

typefaces
Helvetica, Univers

printing technique
Photocopy, Offset Lithography

number of color inks
Three *(sometimes)*

design budget
$178

Picture Perfect

restaurant
Over The Top

location
London, England

designer/illustrator
Tim Davies

copywriter
Nick Jones (*NBJ Leisure*)

year produced
1990

CONCEPT

Over The Top's menu is upbeat, exciting, and reflects the youthful cosmopolitan atmosphere in the restaurant. Illustrated with the restaurant's corporate colors, the menu and restaurant are aimed toward a younger audience.

SPECIAL VISUAL EFFECTS

Strong colors achieve a youthful, fun feeling.

TRENDS FOR THE '90s

"More strongly held to themes but extreme examples emerging, e.g., menus on/made from food (printed on lettuce leaves, etc.) and first weightless restaurants 'Planet Earth,' and 'Space Food.' "

paper stock
Heavy Card Stock

typeface
Hand-scripted

printing technique
Offset Lithography

number of color inks
Four

number produced
1,000 (*first printing*)

design budget
£500

TIM DAVIES

TIM DAVIES

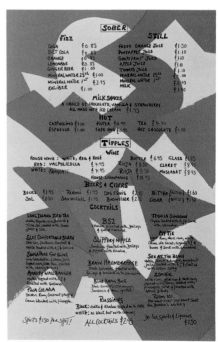

restaurant
Sally's *(Hyatt Regency)*

location
San Diego, California

design firm
Associates Design

art director
Charles Polonsky

designers
Jill Arena
Donna Sommerville

illustrator
Jill Arena

year produced
1992

CONCEPT

Overlooking the San Diego Bay, Sally's
restaurant is known for its fresh seafood.
Sally, the restaurant owner's daughter, is
portrayed in a whimsical and dreamy fashion on each of the restaurant's menus.
Vibrant colors and a loose black line,
prevalent in all three of the unique designs,
lend Mediterranean flavor and tie the
restaurant's theme together. The back of
each menu features ribbon corners to hold
insert sheets.

paper stock
12pt Champion Kromecote C1S

typefaces
Goudy, Kabel

printing technique
Lamination

number of color inks
Four

number produced
1,000 each

restaurant
Cornerstone Grill

location
Brea, California

design firm
On the Edge

designer
Jeff Gasper

illustrator
Ann Field

year produced
1994

CONCEPT

The environment of the Cornerstone Grill combines the best of the overall original structure (brick, dark woods, aged copper) with contemporary design elements such as exaggerated diamond patterns and custom iron railings sculptures, and lighting fixtures. The menu borrows the stone texture, diamond theme and a mural commissioned for the V.I.P room in the restaurant, capturing the upscale mood, subtle colors and high energy of the Cornerstone Grill.

paper stock
Classic Crest Recycled Earthstone

typeface
Matrix

printing technique
Four-color Process

number of color inks
Four

number produced
1,000 *(of each menu)*

restaurant
Metropolis

location
Irvine, California

design firm
On the Edge

designers
Jeff Gasper
Karyn Verdak

year produced
1994

CONCEPT

A fashionable nightclub and billiards hall, Metropolis is an offbeat version of a 1920s club, full of fresh ideas and glamour. The interior design employs golds, purples, clarets and teals set against a black backdrop. The menu design continues this theme. The color scheme, combined with sepia-toned photographs gives the menu a "retro" effect.

paper stock
Evergreen Matte White Recycled

typeface
Custom Hand-drawn

printing technique
Three-color, Metallics

number of color inks
Three

number produced
1,000 *(each menu)*

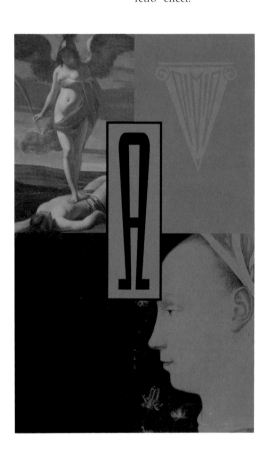

MARTIN FINE PHOTOGRAPHY

88

restaurant
Gotham Hall

location
Santa Monica, California

design firm
On the Edge

designers
Jeff Gasper
Karyn Verdak

year produced
1993

CONCEPT

Located on the second level of the refurbished Odd Fellows Building, Gotham Hall is a billiards nightclub, rich in style and character. The menu design picks up Gotham's interior design by employing the intense tones of purple, green, terra-cotta and metallic touches of its walls. The checkerboard pattern in the carpet is picked up on the menu cover, and is reflected in most of the printed collateral.

paper stock
Evergreen Matte White Recycled

typeface
Matrix Family

printing technique
Four Metallics on Coated Paper

number of color inks
Four Metallics

number produced
1,500

89

restaurant
The Shark Club

location
Costa Mesa, California

design firm
On the Edge

designer
Jeff Gasper

photographer
Joe Mozdzen

year produced
1992

CONCEPT

The Shark Club is an upscale billiards club with dining and bar facilities. One of the main highlights of this appropriately named club is an aquarium filled with several large sharks. The shark that appears on the menu, matchbooks, and business cards is one of the residents of this aquarium.

paper stock
Speckletone "Chord Tone"

typeface
Delta Inline

printing technique
Four-color Process

number of color inks
Four

number produced
2,000

MARTIN FINE PHOTOGRAPHY

restaurant
Bally's Coffee Shop

location
Las Vegas, Nevada

designer/illustrator
Katina R. Loo

copywriter
Paul Contesse

year produced
1992

CONCEPT

Bally's coffee shop menu was designed to become an extension of the several murals that hang in the restaurant.

TRENDS FOR THE '90s

"Menu design should be readable but not boring, designed with visual excitement."

paper stock
**Strathmore Beau Brilliant
130# Mantone Ivory Cover**

typefaces
Futura Book, CG Bodoni, Flora Medium

printing technique
Offset Lithography

number of color inks
Four-color Process

number produced
500

design budget
$1,000

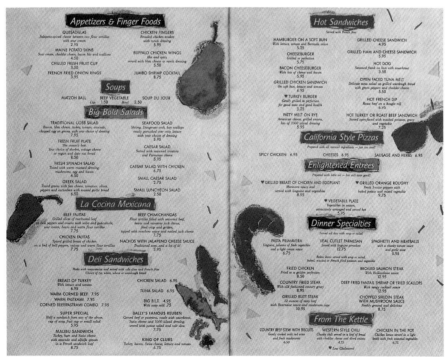

restaurant
The Stinking Rose

location
San Francisco, California

designer/copywriter
Jerry Dal Bozzo

illustrator
Alexander Laurant

year produced
1992

CONCEPT

This menu represents fun, festivity, a party mood, and a restaurant that is dedicated to celebrating the culinary euphoria of garlic. The design expresses abundance, tongue-in-cheek humor and high camp, couched in Surrealistic, 1950s/1960s comic book terms. It was approached from the point of view that garlic is the most important aspect of the restaurant, and there is more garlic at The Stinking Rose than anyone had ever conceived before.

SPECIAL VISUAL EFFECTS

The menu was drawn with a bird's-eye view of the restaurant.

TRENDS FOR THE '90s

"For the past decade, menus have been verbally very descriptive. We believe the trend will be to simplify...menus will continue in the trend to fewer items...with fewer selections in each section. Because there are so many,...restaurants are becoming specialists in one kind of food. They cannot be all things to all people. Menus will reflect this trend. We also believe that menus will be more fun to read because eating out is a recreation for most diners."

paper stock
80# Matrix Gloss Cover

typeface
Times

printing technique
Offset Lithography

number of color inks
Four, Two-color Process

number produced
8,000

design budget
$2,500

92

restaurant
Red Sage

location
Washington, D.C.

design firm
Hasten Design Studios Inc.

designer
Susan Hasten

year produced
1992

CONCEPT

The Red Sage's menu design incorporates typical Western images. Cacti, cowboy boots, and a die-cut steer, which creates an opening in the center of the menu, promote this image.

TRENDS FOR THE '90s

"More fun."

typefaces
CB Univers

number of color inks
One

number produced
1,000

design budget
$20,000 *($3/menu)*

APPETIZERS

Robert's Chorizo & Black Bean Terrine with Fresh Goat Cheese & Avocado Salsa 7.50

Red Sage Sausage en Escabeche 8.50

Chipotle Shrimp on a Buttermilk Corncake 8.75

Fresh Steamed Mussels in Orange Chipotle Broth 9.00

Steak Tartare with Fire Onions and Scotch Bonnet Crema 9.00

Cumin Smoked Swordfish with Baby Artichokes, Orange Cumin Croutons & Roasted Tomato Vinaigrette 11.00

SOUPS & SALADS

Tortilla Soup with Pulled Chicken & Grilled Vegetables 6.50

Chilled Three Tomato Soup 7.00

Mixed Field Greens Salad with Wild Berry Mint Vinaigrette 6.25

Mark's Caesar Salad 6.50

Cinnamon Smoked Quail & Wild Grain Salad with Grilled Sweet Potato Dressing 9.00

Portobello Mushroom Bread 11.00

FROM the SEA

House-Smoked Salmon with Ginger Black Pepper Crust with Red and Yellow Bell Pepper Sauce 19.75

Seared Rare Blackened Tuna with Yellow Mole and Black Bean Sarspadilla Salsa 21.50

Spicy Fried Soft Shell Crabs with Squid Ink Linguini and Peach Salsa 25.00

FROM the BRUSH

Jamaican-Barbequed Chicken Breast and Jerk Chicken Sausage with Fruit & Rum Salsa 17.50

Wood-Roasted Chicken with Chipotle Honey Glaze and Black Bean Chorizo Sauce 18.00

Grilled Duck Breast with Dried Cherry, Habanero Sausage and Blackened Tomato Sauce 19.50

Pan Roasted Quail with Plum Ancho Sauce and a Corn Tamale 21.50

FROM the RANCH

Grilled Pork Loin with Pineapple Habanero Salsa and Spicy Pork Tamale 17.50

Double Pecan Chile Lamb Chop with Smoked Lamb Sausage and Goat Cheese Mashed Potatoes 23.00

Peppered Beef Tenderloin with Roasted Corn Relish and Wild Mushroom Chile de Arbol Sauce 24.00

Cowboy Ribeye Steak with Barbeque Black Beans & Chile Onion Rings 27.50

FROM the GARDEN

Wild Mushroom Risotto with Roasted Corn, Pearl Onions and Baked Parmesan 16.00

Vegetarian Plate: Corn Tamale, Goat Cheese Mashed Potatoes, Fried Spinach with Fresh Seasonal Vegetables 16.50

For the dining comfort and privacy of our guests, the taking of pictures is prohibited.
Please, no pipes or cigars.
An 18% gratuity may be added to parties of 6 or more.

BY the GLASS

	glass	bottle
SPARKLING		
Gruet, Brut, New Mexico N.V.	5.25	24.50
Charles Heidsieck Brut N.V.	7.00	31.00
WHITE		
Red Sage's White Wine, "Viento Secco" made for us by Carmenet	4.50	18.00
Gewurztraminer, Claiborne & Churchill Central Coast 1991	4.95	19.50
Chardonnay, Guenoc, "Treasure the Chesapeake", Napa 1991	5.75	23.00
Chardonnay, Iron Horse "Cuvee Joy", Sonoma 1990	7.50	30.00
RED		
Red Sage Red	4.50	20.00
Lyeth, Alexander Valley 1988	5.25	21.00
Grenache, "Clos de Gilroy" Bonny Doon, Santa Cruz 1992	5.50	22.00

restaurant
Aureole

location
New York, New York

designer
Charles Palmer

illustrator
Mark Hess

year produced
1988

CONCEPT

Vibrant colors and surreal images bring Aureole's dessert menu to life. The use of a satin varnish gives the illustration significant meaning.

TRENDS FOR THE '90s

"Understated, clean and easily accessible."

Aureole's Desserts

Cool Caramel Mousse with Cinnamon Basted Fruits
raisin spice cake, pulled sugar basket and creme anglaise

Maple Roasted Pear Delice with Warm Pear Fritters
smooth maple mousse and brandy laced sabayon

Granny Smith Apple Gateau with Toasted Streusel
crisps of baked apple and fresh lemon ice cream

Bittersweet Chocolate and Toasted Cashew Torte
with crisp cashew meringue, cashew ice cream and milk chocolate spheres

Double Lemon Tartlet with Citrus Pudding
caramel sugar crisp and english cream

Malted Mocha and Chocolate Parfait
with a sour cream ice cream and deep chocolate bar

Classic Crème Brulée
with linzer biscuits

A Service of Market Fruits and Trilevel Sorbet
natural nectars

Three Select Cheeses Paired with a Honey Roasted Pear Terrine
and toasted sourdough walnut bread

Fresh Raspberries ($4.00 supp.)
or
Strawberries
sweet cream, creme fraiche, or creme chantilly

Ice Creams, Sorbets

Desserts $7.00
Coffee $2.50
Espresso & Cappuccino $3.00

Aureole's Hand Made Specialty Chocolates
By the Pound
1/2 lb—$28
1/4 lb—$14

printing technique
Four-color Process

number of color inks
Five

number produced
20,000

design budget
$31,200 *($1.56 per piece)*

restaurant
Tropicana Hotel and Casino
(Food and Beverage Department)

location
Las Vegas, Nevada

design firm
Kenyon Press

designer
John Wu

year produced
1991

CONCEPT

The menu allows for maximum flexibility, as the number and types of inserts enclosed in the menu can be easily changed, depending on the menu's recipient. The die-cut palm trees prevent noticeable gaps.

SPECIAL VISUAL EFFECTS

The folder's vibrant artwork is representative of the Tropicana Hotel and Casino, in its colorful and contemporary design.

TRENDS FOR THE '90s

"Menus that allow interchangeable components will lead the industry. It keeps the menu fresh and reduces the cost of production."

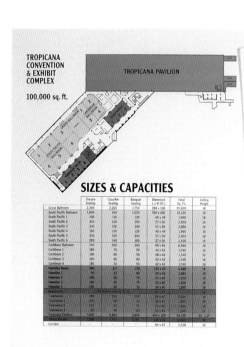

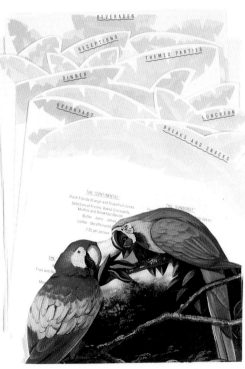

SIZES & CAPACITIES

	Theatre Seating	Class-Rm Seating	Banquet Seating	Dimension L x W (Ft.)	Total Sq. Ft.	Ceiling Height
Grand Ballroom	2,300	2,265	1,750	288 x 100	25,830	16
South Pacific Ballroom	1,600	810	1,020	156 x 100	15,120	16
South Pacific 1	190	110	120	40 x 49	1,960	16
South Pacific 2	310	150	200	57 x 50	2,850	16
South Pacific 3	310	150	200	57 x 50	2,850	16
South Pacific 4	190	110	120	40 x 49	1,960	16
South Pacific 5	310	150	200	57 x 50	2,850	16
South Pacific 6	290	140	180	57 x 50	2,650	16
Caribbean Ballroom	740	300	360	90 x 64	6,960	16
Caribbean 1	180	70	90	42 x 42	1,740	16
Caribbean 2	190	80	90	48 x 42	1,340	16
Caribbean 3	190	80	90	42 x 42	1,740	16
Caribbean 4	180	70	90	42 x 42	1,740	16
Havelbar Room	390	217	270	120 x 40	4,640	16
Havelbar 1	90	52	60	30 x 26	1,080	16
Havelbar 2	100	55	70	30 x 40	1,200	16
Havelbar 3	100	55	70	30 x 40	1,200	16
Havelbar 4	100	55	70	30 x 40	1,200	16
Boardroom				30 x 140		
Tradewinds	290	154	200	39 x 40	1,600	16
Tradewinds 1	100	70	70	40 x 40	1,200	16
Tradewinds 2	100	70	70	30 x 40	1,200	16
Tradewinds 3	95	48	65	33 x 30	1,000	16
Tropicana Pavilion	7,800	6,840	3,650	456 x 120	54,720	33 1/2'
	1,200	1,150		145 x 92	12,400	16
Corridor				84 x 42	3,528	16

TROPICANA CONVENTION & EXHIBIT COMPLEX
100,000 sq. ft.
TROPICANA PAVILION

BREAKS AND SNACKS

THE "CONTINENTAL"
Fresh Florida Orange and Grapefruit Juices
Selection of Freshly Baked Croissants,
Muffins and Breakfast Danish
Butter   Jams   Jellies
Coffee   Decaffeinated   Tea
7.25 per person

THE "SUNBURST"
Fresh Florida Orange and Grapefruit Juices
Display of Sliced Seasonal Fruits
Selection of Freshly Baked Croissants,
Muffins and Breakfast Danish
Butter   Jams   Jellies
Coffee   Decaffeinated   Tea
8.25 per person

THE "HEALTHBREAK"
Assorted Yogurts
Fruit and Nut Breads   Cream Cheese
Fresh Whole Fruit
Mineral Water and Fruit Juices
7.50 per person

THE "SPORTSBREAK"
Hot Dogs
Popcorn
Potato Chips
Diet and Regular Soft Drinks
8.50 per person

THE "SWEET TOOTH"
Assorted Fancy Cookies
Fresh Brownies
Ice Cream Station
Soft Drinks, Coffee, Tea and Milk
8.50 per person

Prices do not include local tax and gratuity.

restaurant
One Market Restaurant

location
San Francisco, California

designers
Claude Jacques
Michael D. Dellar
Bradley Ogden

illustrator
Mercedes McDonald

copywriters
Michael D. Dellar
Bradley Ogden

year produced
1993

CONCEPT

One Market Restaurant offers farm-fresh
American fare and all-American wines in a
bustling cosmopolitan environment.
Menus are modular and flexible, and
change daily. The design concept utilizes
Mercedes McDonald's artwork as a cover
in a plastic sleeve in which the daily menus
and wine lists are inserted. There are seven
different menu covers. All printing was
done on a color copier for speed of turn
around and initial cost control. The original artwork has been framed and adorns
the restaurant's two private dining rooms.

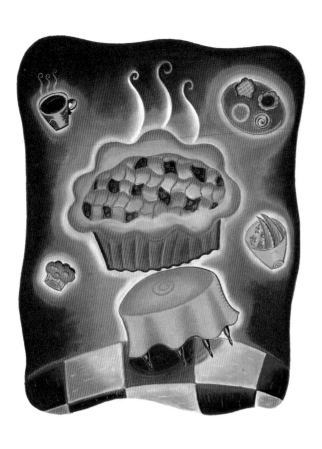

TRENDS FOR THE '90s

"Trends toward flexibility and simplicity in design, allowing the restaurant to change quickly when the product changes."

paper stock
Standard Copier Paper

printing technique
**Laserjet Color Copier
Jet Printer**

number produced
101 of each menu

design budget
**$1,500 plastic covers
$3,500 Art
$1,500 Production**

restaurant
Harvest Restaurant

location
Cambridge, Massachusetts

design firm
Clifford Selbert Design, Inc.

designer
Melanie Lowe

illustrators
Mark Fisher *(Dessert)*
Melanie Lowe *(Large Menu)*

photographer
Susie Cushner *(Small & Large Menus)*

year produced
1993

CONCEPT
Harvest Restaurant is an eclectic restaurant
that changes its menu monthly.
Adaptable menus for the restaurant's four
styles of offerings were designed, each
using a different photo or illustration to
play up the artichoke logo.

TRENDS FOR THE '90s
"Menus will become personalized to the
specific type of restaurant and also be more
adaptable for changing styles of dining."

paper stock
Champion Kromecote Recycled

typefaces
Bold *(headlines)*
Regular *(body)*

printing technique
Offset with Matte Laminate Coating

number of color inks
Four

number produced
500 of each

design budget
$2,500 plus trade agreement

restaurant
Mario Italian Restaurant

location
Hong Kong

design firm
McCann Erickson (HK) Ltd

creative director
Kitty Lun

designers
Joel Chu
Tom Tong

illustrator
Tom Tong

photographer
Victor Hung

copywriter
Kitty Lun

year produced
1993

CONCEPT

The menu's modern, colorful, vibrant design reflects the casual Italian dining atmosphere of Mario Italian Restaurant. The cover's illustration style communicates freedom. The use of food and ingredients of Italian dishes as illustration subjects enhances appetite appeal. On the inside pages, photographs of ingredients and dishes are fully integrated within the over-all menu design.

TRENDS FOR THE '90s

"I predict more breakthrough in menu designs in the '90s—not just in graphics, but also in the size, shape, medium used and presentation. Customers go into a restaurant not just for the food but the total dining experience. The menu is almost the first thing they encounter. It will set the mood for the rest of the meal. Many restaurateurs and designers will be able to see this trend and we will soon see a lot more bold ideas in their designs."

paper stock
Matte Art Paper 420gsm

typeface
Weiss

printing technique
Offset Lithography

number produced
3,000

restaurant
Cafe S.F.A. *(Saks Fifth Avenue)*

location
San Francisco, California

design firm
Associates Design

art director
Charles Polonsky

designers
Jill Arena
Donna Sommerville

illustrators
Jill Arena
Roberta Serafini *(mailer)*

CONCEPT

Developed for Saks Fifth Avenue Cafes, the
S.F.A. Collection uses a sophisticated color
palette, medium-colored pencil on dark
paper and gold stamping to portray high-
fashion and culture.

The rich hues in the illustrations were
selected from the cafe's actual dinnerware
pattern and the backgrounds incorporate
each cities' distinctive skyline, capturing a
cosmopolitan essence.

paper stock
Neenah Classic Linen

typeface
Globe Gothic

printing technique
Four-color Process, Gold Stamping

number of color inks
Four

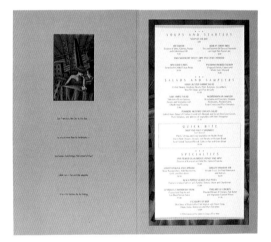

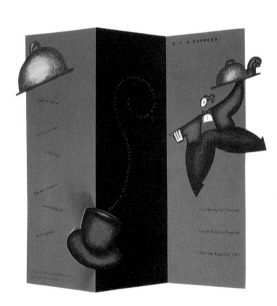

restaurant
Moose's

location
San Francisco, California

designer/illustrator
Ward Schumaker

year produced
1992

CONCEPT

For this eponymous restaurant owned by celebrities Mary Etta and Ed Moose, a logo was created that features a handwritten *Moose's*, in which the letters *o* function as the eyes of a silly looking moose. The moose logo is incorporated throughout the graphics program.

TRENDS FOR THE '90s

" 'Significant trends' annoy me terrifically, whether I'm forced to look at them or am asked to provide artwork which fits in with them. I try to do as little of both as possible."

paper stock
Champion Kromecote
Simpson Evergreen
Strathmore Writing

typefaces
Calligraphy, Berkeley

printing technique
Offset Lithography

number of color inks
Two

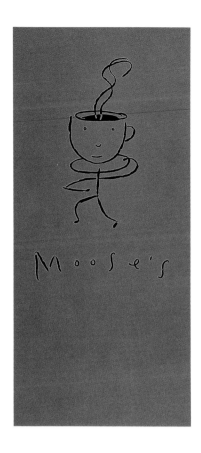

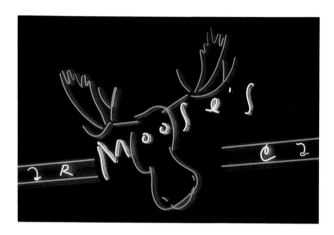

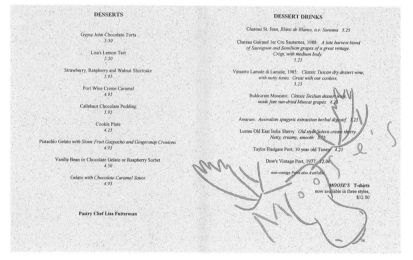

DESSERTS

Gypsy John Chocolate Torta
5.50

Lisa's Lemon Tart
5.50

Strawberry, Raspberry and Walnut Shortcake
5.95

Port Wine Creme Caramel
4.95

Callebaut Chocolate Pudding
3.95

Cookie Plate
4.25

Pistachio Gelato with *Stone Fruit Gazpacho and Gingersnap Croutons*
4.95

Vanilla Bean or Chocolate Gelato or Raspberry Sorbet
4.50

Gelato with *Chocolate-Caramel Sauce*
4.95

Pastry Chef Lisa Futterman

DESSERT DRINKS

Chateau St. Jean, *Blanc de Blancs, n.v. Sonoma* 5.25

Chateau Guiraud 1er Cru Sauternes, 1988: *A late harvest blend of Sauvignon and Semillion grapes of a great vintage. Crisp, with medium body.*
5.25

Vinsanto Lamole di Lamole, 1985: *Classic Tuscan dry dessert wine, with nutty tones. Great with our cookies.*
3.25

Bukkuram Moscato: *Classic Sicilian dessert wine, made fom sun-dried Muscat grapes* 4.25

Amarum: *Australian spagyric extraction herbal digestif* 3.25

Lustau Old East India Sherry: *Old style Soleria cream sherry. Nutty, creamy, smooth* 3.95

Taylor Fladgate Port, 10 year old Tawny 4.25

Dow's Vintage Port, 1977 12.00

non-vintage Ports also Available

MOOSE'S T-shirts
now available in three styles,
$12.00

restaurant
Carnival Cruise Lines *(Headquarters)*

location
Miami, Florida

design firm
Associates Design

art director
Charles Polonsky

designers
Jill Arena
Donna Sommerville

illustrator
Jill Arena

year produced
1992 & 1993

CONCEPT

Devised to coordinate with special on-board events, these half-fold menus convey specific themes.

A vibrant oil pastel drawing of a bullfighter is used to symbolize a Latin celebration in the Viva **España**! menu. Handmade paper embellished in the rich *Caribbean Evening* watercolor painting is portrayed on the Caribbean Calypso menu cover. "Adventure" is reflected in the Westward Passage menu, using an authentic and aged style of a fifteenth-century exploration ship. The Farewell menu depicts the Carnival Cruise ship in a moody acrylic painting.

paper stock
Neenah Classic Linen

typefaces
Americana
Goudy Old-style
Garamond
Barcelona

printing technique
Offset Lithography

number of color inks
Four-color Process

BREAKFAST EXPRESS

GOOD MORNING

Please Hang On Door Handle by 2:00 a.m.

Name _____

Room Number _____

Number of Guests _____

Please Circle Desired Service Time

6:30-6:45 a.m.   7:15-7:30 a.m.   8:15-8:30 a.m.
6:45-7:00 a.m.   7:30-7:45 a.m.   8:30-8:45 a.m.
7:00-7:15 a.m.   7:45-8:00 a.m.   8:45-9:00 a.m.
                   8:00-8:15 a.m.

☐ THE CONTINENTAL 6.95
Choose one from each category:
Juice   ☐ Orange ☐ Grapefruit
Toast   ☐ Wheat   ☐ White ☐ Rye
          ☐ Buttered ☐ Unbuttered
          or
          ☐ Basket of Breakfast Baked Goods
Beverage ☐ Coffee ☐ Decaffeinated
          ☐ Milk   ☐ Tea

☐ THE AMERICAN 9.95
Choose one from each category:
Fruit   ☐ Melon   ☐ Half Grapefruit
or
Juice   ☐ Orange ☐ Grapefruit
Two Jumbo
Eggs   ☐ Scrambled ☐ Poached ☐ Fried
Meat   ☐ Bacon   ☐ Link Sausage ☐ Ham
Toast   ☐ Wheat   ☐ White ☐ Rye
          ☐ Buttered ☐ Unbuttered
          or
          ☐ Basket of Breakfast Baked Goods
Beverage ☐ Coffee ☐ Decaffeinated
          ☐ Milk   ☐ Tea

☐ ULTRA SLIM-FAST®
          ☐ Vanilla Shake 2.95
          ☐ Chocolate Shake 2.95
          ☐ Strawberry Shake 2.95
Requests: _____
          _____
          _____

For complete breakfast orders, refer to our Room Service Menu.
$1.50 per room delivery charge, 5% D.C. Sales Tax and
15% gratuity will be added to your bill.

WASHINGTON, D.C.
RENAISSANCE
HOTEL

restaurant
Ramada Renaissance Hotels and Resorts

location
Coral Gables, Florida

design firm
Associates Design

art director
Charles Polonsky

designers
Roberta Serafini
Jill Arena
Donna Sommerville

illustrator
Roberta Serafini

year produced
1993

CONCEPT

Each of these "morning breakfast" designs are tailored to appeal to the different locations of Renaissance Hotels and Resorts, from warm and country-like themes to urban themes.

SPECIAL VISUAL EFFECTS

Country-like themes come across through the use of a photograph in the design; urban themes through contemporary illustration.

paper stock
12pt Carolina Cover C1S

typeface
Garamond

printing technique
Offset Lithography

number of color inks
Four

RENAISSANCE

Breakfast

restaurant
Heinemann's Restaurants

location
Milwaukee, Wisconsin

design firm
Rachel Stephens Design

designer
Rachel Stephens

illustrator
Keith Ward

copywriter
Sandy Shaw

year produced
1991

CONCEPT
The design communicates quality and the extent to which the restaurant goes to assure the customer is served the best food possible.

SPECIAL VISUAL EFFECTS
The cover illustration emphasizes natural ingredients without making Heinemann's appear to be a "health food" restaurant.

paper stock
110# Gilbert Esse Grover Smooth

typefaces
Cheltennam, Baskerville

printing technique
Offset Lithography

number of color inks
Five

number produced
5,000 each

design budget
$10,000

SANDWICHES

All of our sandwiches are prepared with breads made by us in our own bakery. We use only the finest natural ingredients and no preservatives. *Choose from:* white, whole wheat, rye, English Muffin, Health (whole wheat, oatmeal, sunflower seeds and honey), Welsh (whole wheat, pumpernickel and more).

CHICKEN SALAD
We carefully cook our chicken daily with a special combination of herbs and spices blended together with Hellmann's mayonnaise $4.50

ALBACORE TUNA SALAD
Water-packed tuna (dolphin safe!) blended with the finest herbs and Hellmann's mayonnaise $4.50

CRUNCHY CHICKEN OR TUNA SALAD
Served on our own health bread with almonds, sprouts, tomato and a hint of chutney! $4.95

OUR SPECIAL CLUB
Sliced turkey, chicken salad, egg salad, or tuna salad with our special cure bacon, tomato, lettuce and mayonnaise on your choice of home-made toast $4.95

GRILLED ALASKAN COD SANDWICH (h)
A wonderfully mild fillet on a home-made bun with lettuce, tomato and just the right touch of almonds and seasoned margarine $4.50

A GREAT HOT DOG
The best all beef hot dog we could find! $2.25

HEINEMANN'S BAGEL SPECIAL
Sliced turkey, cream cheese, tomato and lettuce on a toasted bagel $4.50

JAMAICA GRILL
Bacon, onion, tomato and Swiss cheese on Welsh bread $4.50

MENDOCINO GRILL (h)
Sliced turkey, mozzarella cheese, tomato and chutney on health bread $4.75

KAHLER GRILL
Aged cheddar cheese, green pepper, and bacon grilled on Welsh bread $4.50

THE PLATTER
Hungry? Add hash browns, mashed potatoes, french fries or Heinemann's house salad to any of the sandwiches . . . $1.00

GRILLED SPECIALTIES

Our own sensational ground USDA Steak Burger or Turkey Burgers are grilled to order and served on a home-made unbleached white or stone ground (by us!) whole wheat bun.

THE GOURMET
Bacon, bleu cheese and tomato (also raw onions!)
Steak Burger $4.45
Ground Turkey $4.45

ARIZONA
Covered with tangy barbeque sauce and our own special cure bacon.
Steak Burger $3.95
Ground Turkey $3.95

SWISS (h)
Chopped green olives and melted imported Swiss cheese.
Steak Burger $3.95
Ground Turkey $3.95

CALIFORNIA
Lettuce, tomato and 1000 Island dressing.
Steak Burger $3.95
Ground Turkey $3.95

BLEU CHEESE
A great treat for the connoisseur!
Steak Burger $3.95
Ground Turkey $3.95

WISCONSIN CHEESE
Your choice of American, house-aged cheddar or mozzarella cheese.
Steak Burger $3.75
Ground Turkey $3.75

JUST PLAIN GRILLED (h)
With or without fried onions.
Steak Burger $3.50
Ground Turkey $3.50

HEINEMANN'S SPECIAL GRILL
Nestled between Swiss and American cheese with just a hint of onion, then grilled on Welsh bread.
Steak Burger $3.95
Ground Turkey $3.95

THE PLATTER
Hungry? Add hash browns, mashed potatoes, french fries or Heinemann's house salad to any of the Grilled Specialties $1.00

HEINEMANN'S FAVORITES

GRILLED ALASKAN COD
A hit at Heinemann's! It is served with an herb and almond butter, your choice of potatoes, and toast . $5.95

TURKEY AND BROCCOLI (h)
For a light, nutritious treat, try this combination of sliced hot turkey breast on top of Welsh bread, covered with a flavorful herbed sauce and Swiss cheese, tucked with fresh broccoli. Low calorie and delicious! $4.95

OLD FASHIONED CHICKEN POT PIE
Perennially popular! Diced home-cooked chicken in a creamy sauce with potatoes and vegetables, topped with a home-made flaky pie crust $4.75

FRIED SHRIMP
¼ pound of premium gulf shrimp fried to order. Served with choice of potatoes, garnish and home-made toast . $4.75

GOLDEN WAFFLE SUPREME
Our fluffy, tender specialty is served with real maple syrup $3.10

Add Heinemann's house salad to any of the favorites $1.00

SIDE ORDERS

OUR WONDERFUL ONION RINGS
A short stack $1.50
Mound $1.95

POTATOES
Hash brown, mashed potatoes or french fries $1.10

OUR FAMOUS GRILLED COFFEE CAKE
Home-made and featured in National Geographic Magazine! $1.25

GRILLED HOME-MADE BRAN BREAD
With cinnamon sugar. It's terrific! . . $1.25

SALADS

OUR FABULOUS HOME-MADE CHICKEN SALAD
Each day, we tenderly cook chicken with a blend of herbs and spices, then blend it with Hellmann's mayonnaise. Served on lettuce, it comes with your choice of one of our home-made toasted breads $5.50

ALBACORE TUNA SALAD PLATE
Water packed tuna (dolphin safe!) blended with Hellmann's and served as above $5.50

HEINEMANN'S HEALTH SALAD (h)
Julienne turkey breast, imported Swiss cheese, fresh vegetables and sunflower seeds on a base of fresh greens, with a slice of home-made toast $5.50

AUDUBON SCOOP
For a lighter appetite, try this! A scoop of our terrific chicken or tuna salad on lettuce, with garnish and a slice of home-made toast $3.95

HEINEMANN'S HOUSE SALAD . $1.95

BEVERAGES

OUR COFFEE
We pride ourselves in having the finest coffee obtainable anywhere in the world! Our own special blend that is freshly ground seconds before it is brewed . . . . . . 85¢

OUR SPECIAL BLEND TEA
We also created our own special blend of tea. Served hot or iced . . . . 85¢

MILK
2%, Skim or Chocolate . . . . . 85¢/$1.10

MALTS & SHAKES
Prepared with generous scoops of our thick, creamy ice cream. We use real malt powder for that delicious, old-fashioned taste in our malts. With our own home-made ice cream $2.25

STRAWBERRY HEALTH SHAKE (h)
Made with our fabulous strawberry/banana yogurt, orange juice and fresh bananas $2.25

LEMONADE . . . . 95¢

PEPSI, DIET PEPSI, SLICE, ORANGE SLICE *(FREE REFILLS)* . . . . 95¢

DINNER SPECIALTIES

In addition to our terrific nightly specials, the following favorites are available from 4:00 p.m. in our suburban restaurants on their respective nights and include a choice of soup or salad.

MONDAY
Spaghetti and Meat Sauce. . . This wonderful sauce is gently simmered for hours. Served with garlic bread and garnish $5.50

TUESDAY
Madeira Chicken. . . Grilled to order and served over a vegetable wild rice blend. Topped with a terrific Madeira wine sauce. With choice of toast and garnish . . . $5.95

WEDNESDAY
Old Fashioned Meat Loaf. . . This Heinemann's recipe is decades old! We make it with US choice ground sirloin and all natural ingredients that include a special combination of herbs, garlic and onion. Served open-faced on your choice of home-made bread with mashed potatoes and hearth gravy $6.95

THURSDAY
Joe's Lasagna. . . This mouth-watering lasagna is made with spinach, pasta, mozzarella cheese and a thick meat sauce. Along with good taste, it's also low in fat $5.95

FRIDAY
Our Fabulous Fish Fry. . . Beer battered Alaskan Cod served with a choice of potatoes, cole slaw and marble rye bread $6.95

SATURDAY
Hunter's Chicken. . . One-half chicken roasted with herbs and served with a mushroom, carrot, and onion "Hunter's Sauce." With choice of potatoes, toast and garnish $6.50

SUNDAY
Grilled Pork Medallions. . . Two boneless pork chops grilled to order and topped with a light wine sauce. Served with choice of potatoes, toast and garnish $6.95

(h) Indicates especially nutritious items that are prepared to be low in fat and calories!

EGGS

All of our farm fresh eggs are Grade A extra large and served with your choice of our own home-made toasted bread. *Choose from:* white, rye, stone ground whole wheat (we grind it ourselves!), Health (whole wheat, oatmeal, sunflower seeds, and honey), Welsh (a sensational combination of whole wheat, pumpernickel, and more), English Muffin (has no fat), and Raisin.

OMELETS
Choose any two of the following: Ham, bacon, cheese, onion, green pepper, or mushroom $4.25

HEINEMANN'S SPECIAL
The #1 breakfast in Milwaukee! Two scrambled eggs, plus diced ham . . $3.75

NORTHWOODS
Two eggs, any style, with your choice of turkey sausage, bacon, or pork sausage and hash brown potatoes $4.75

FARM STYLE
Two eggs, any style, with bacon or sausage and your choice of toast $3.95

FAST STARTER
One fresh egg, any style, with hash brown potatoes $2.40

SUSIE'S SPECIAL
Grilled home-made turkey sausage, topped with a freshly fried egg, sprinkled with aged cheddar cheese, and served on a toasted English Muffin $3.75

SIDE ORDERS

HASH BROWN POTATOES $1.10
BACON $1.85
PORK SAUSAGE $1.85
OUR OWN HOME-MADE TURKEY SAUSAGE PATTY (h)
Low fat! $1.95

LIGHT STARTS

High in nutrition and low in cholesterol.

BREAKFAST OF THE 90'S
Zero cholesterol eggs, home-made turkey sausage, hash brown potatoes, and stone ground whole wheat toast $4.95

BETTER THAN EGGS! (h)
Our special flavorful egg substitute.
Equivalent of 2 eggs $2.50
Equivalent of 1 egg $1.95
Omelet (with any two ingredients) $4.50

BREAKFAST SUNDAE (h)
Lovely layers of fresh fruit, home-made granola, raisins and yogurt. Great! $3.10

ENERGY BREAKFAST (h)
A terrific mixture of oatmeal, apples and yogurt, topped with home-made granola and fresh fruit $2.95

STRAWBERRY HEALTH SHAKE (h)
Made with our fabulous Strawberry-Banana yogurt, orange juice and fresh bananas $2.50

SEASONAL FRESH FRUIT CUP (h) . . . $2.25

HEINEMANN'S BAKED OATMEAL (h)
A baked ensemble of Irish oatmeal, cinnamon, brown sugar, vanilla and more. Raisins optional! $2.25

OATMEAL WITH THE WORKS (h)
With home-made granola, brown sugar and raisins $2.10

IRISH OATMEAL (h) $1.50

SELECTION OF COLD CEREAL (h) . . . $1.50

BANANAS WITH ANY OF THE ABOVE . . . . Please add 50¢

PANCAKES & MORE

PANCAKES
Very light, and served with our own maple syrup $3.25

WILD BLUEBERRY PANCAKES
Our wonderful pancakes made with wild Maine blueberries $4.10

OATMEAL PANCAKES
Home-made with our own Irish Oatmeal and served with maple syrup $3.50

WAFFLE
A favorite for generations! It is golden, hot and crisp, served with maple syrup . . $3.25

FRENCH TOAST
Your choice of bread grilled, sprinkled with powdered sugar and served with maple syrup $3.25

JOGGER'S FRENCH TOAST
Home-made health bread grilled and topped with sliced bananas, yogurt and granola $4.25

SPECIALTIES

GRILLED COFFEE CAKE
Laced with cinnamon, raisins, butter and more. This fabulous treat was featured in National Geographic Magazine! $1.25

GRILLED HOME-MADE BRAN BREAD
With cinnamon sugar. It's terrific! . $1.25

HOME-MADE TOAST (h)
Your choice of our own breads, served with preserves . . . . 95¢

HOME-MADE MUFFINS (h)
We make them ourselves with no preservatives. Oat Bran, Banana, or Health Nut $1.10

ENGLISH MUFFIN (h) $1.25

BAGEL (h) $1.25
With cream cheese $1.75

(h) Indicates especially nutritious items that are prepared to be low in fat and calories!

SPECIALS

HEINEMANN'S BREAKFAST BAKE

SAUSAGE, HAM, POTATOES,
EGGS AND CHEESE
BAKED WITH ONIONS, MUSHROOMS
AND GREEN PEPPERS
SERVED WITH HOME-MADE SALSA
AND CHOICE OF TOAST!

$4.25

COFFEE

OUR COFFEE
We pride ourselves in having the finest coffee obtainable anywhere in the world! Our own special blend that is freshly ground seconds before it is served . . .85¢

BEVERAGES

ORANGE JUICE . . . . 95¢
GRAPEFRUIT JUICE . . . . 95¢
MILK All Types . . . . 85¢/$1.10
TEA
Our own special blend, or herbed . . . 85¢
HOT CHOCOLATE . . . . 75¢

OUR HANDMADE
CANDIES AWAIT YOU...

Step up to the front of the store
and delight in an incredible taste treat.
From our Copper Kettle Caramels
to our Chocolate Covered Grahams, you'll enjoy
a time-honored tradition in quality.
All of our candies are made from scratch
with the finest, all-natural ingredients.
Sweet creamery butter, farmer's cream, and
imported Bourbon vanilla are but a few.
Take our exclusive candies with you
or fill out an order card, and we'll send them to you.
They also make very special gifts!

Heinemann's
NATURALLY GOOD QUALITY SINCE 1923.

Heinemann's
NATURALLY GOOD QUALITY SINCE 1923.

restaurant
Garibaldi

location
Conrad, Puerta Vallarta, Mexico

design firm
Kenyon Press

designer/illustrator
Dick Witt

year produced
1992

CONCEPT

Located directly on the beach with an open-air thatched-roof construction, Garibaldi has a lively, colorful Latin theme. The wait staff serve in matador-style uniforms to the sound of Latin music. The menu design reflects Garibaldi's personality and is both durable and flexible, allowing for daily changes.

SPECIAL VISUAL EFFECTS

The logo was illustrated into the scene in the same style to preserve the overall look. The black fields were hand-etched at the film stage to add density and depth.

TRENDS FOR THE '90s

"Sophisticated laser-compatibility and durability."

paper stock
14pt Carolina C1S

printing technique
Sheet-fed

number of color inks
Four-color Process

number produced
500

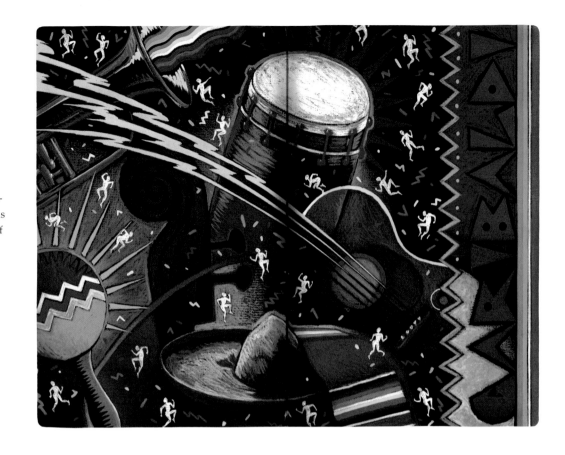

restaurant
Bistro 100

location
Chicago, Illinois

design firm
The Levy Restaurants

art director
Marcy Lansing

illustrator
Judy Rifka

year produced
1992

CONCEPT

The menu design and various printed materials are taken from a detail of a mural that was commissioned for Bistro 100. Interior shells were printed in one color, and given to the restaurant to print in-house on their laser printer.

TRENDS FOR THE '90s

"Many of our menus are housed in plastic covers made of laminated vinyl for longevity of the menus, and are printed with the flexibility of 'printing shells' that print from one to three colors. The shells are given to the restaurants to print in-house on their laser printers."

paper stock
Warren Lustro Dull Cream Enamel *(cover)*
Hopper 60# Skytone *(text)*
Hopper/Natural *(inserts, shells)*

number of color inks
Four-color Process *(cover)*
One PMS *(inside, shells)*

5

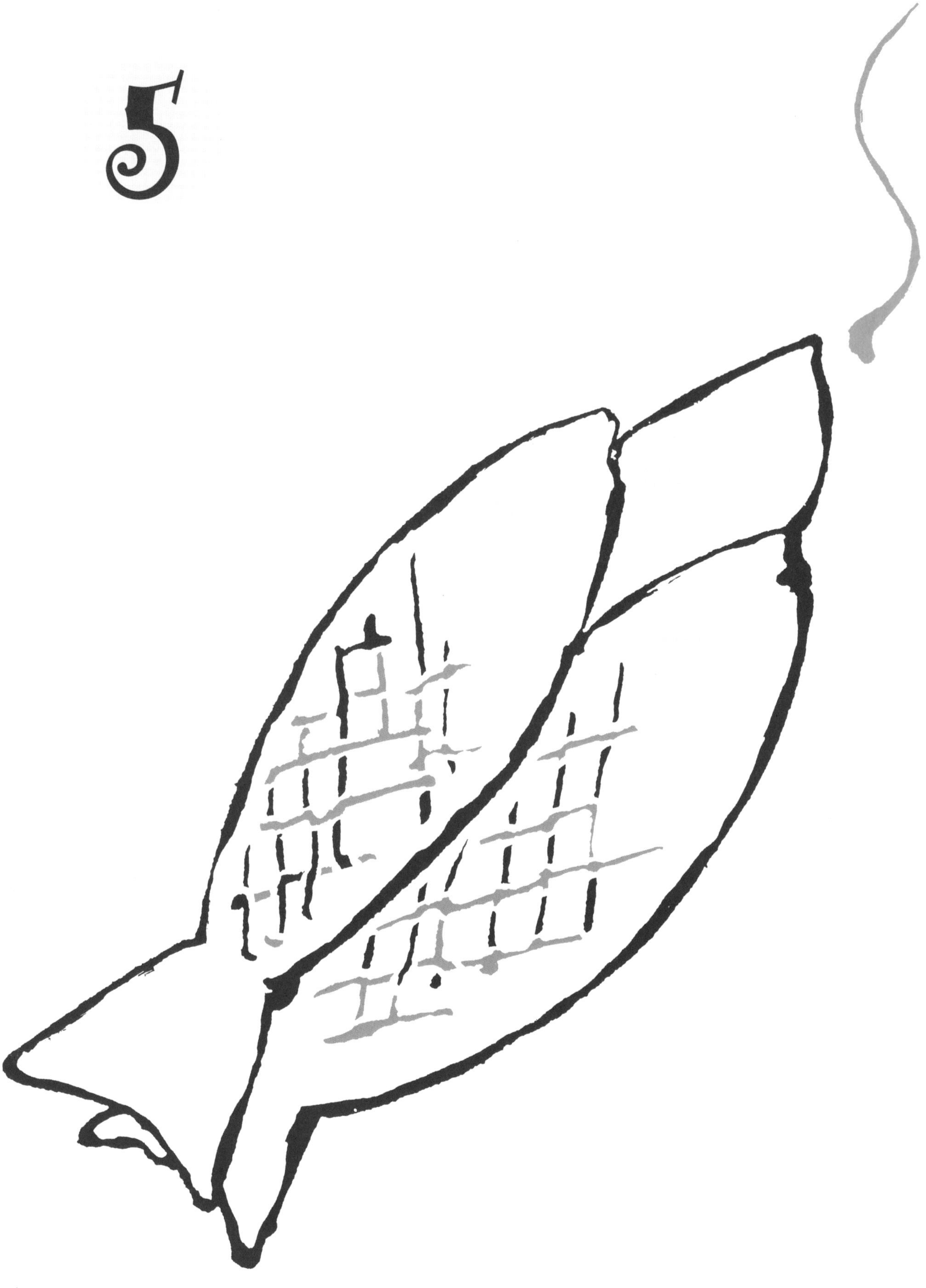

Seven Seas

restaurant
The Beach Club

location
Rockaway Beach, New York

design firm
Presentations, Ltd.

designer
Tom Vlahakis

illustrator
Eric Karalis

copywriter
Steve Good

year produced
1994

CONCEPT

The Beach Club overlooks the beach and the Atlantic Ocean, and is decorated throughout with surfboards. The menu design reflects the theme of this restaurant with a humorous approach. Playful illustrations, such as egg characters surfing on bacon slices in the breakfast menu and a comical shark swimming throughout the main menu make these menus both interesting and fun.

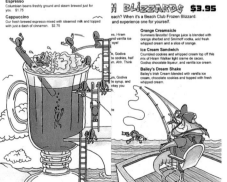

THE BEACH CLUB

OFF PREMISE
CATERING MENU

129 BEACH 116 ST. ROCKAWAY BEACH, N.Y. 11694 718-634-6500

THE BEACH CLUB

BREAKFAST MENU

COLD BUFFET
Includes Choice of 2 salads and 3 deluxe salads
and a Fresh Cold Cut Platter

SALADS
FRESH VEGETABLE SALAD · CUCUMBER SALAD
CAESAR SALAD · POTATO SALAD
MACARONI SALAD · COLE SLAW

DELUXE SALADS
DIJON TORTELLINI SALAD · PASTA PRIMAVERA
CHICKEN SALAD · TUNA SALAD
CAJUN CHICKEN SALAD
SHRIMP SALAD · CHOPPED EGG SALAD
MOZZARELLA and TOMATOES · CRAB SALAD
SEAFOOD PASTA SALAD

FRESH COLD CUT PLATTER
Featuring Boars Head Cold Cuts

ROAST BEEF · TURKEY BREAST · CORNED BEEF
VIRGINIA HAM · SWISS and AMERICAN CHEESE

Also Includes: Fresh Baked Rolls, Rye Bread, White Bread,
Plates, Forks, Knives, Napkins, Serving Utensils, Mustard and Mayonnaise.
Delivered & Set Up, Ready To Serve On Your Table.
$6.95 per person
(20 person minimum)

WESTERN BBQ COOKOUT
An All Inclusive Outdoor Barbecue.
We Manage Everything Including Delivery, Set Up, Cooking, Serving and
Cleanup. All You Have to do is Relax and Enjoy the Party.

HOT DOG   CORN ON THE COB
HAMBURGER   WATERMELON
SAUSAGE & PEPPERS   POTATO SALAD
BABY BACK RIBS   COLE SLAW
BBQ CHICKEN   BREAD & ROLLS
BAKED BEANS   SODAS & LEMONADE

Also Includes: Plastic Forks, Knives, Spoons, Dinner Plates, Napkins,
Serving Utensils and Table Cloths.
Priced According To Size Of Party.

HOT & COLD BUFFET
Choice of:
· 1 Salad and 1 Deluxe Salad · Fresh Cold Cut Platter
· 1 Hot Pasta or Rice · Choice of 2 Hot Entrees
· Fresh Baked Bread and Rolls
$9.95 per person

HOT BUFFET
Choice of:
· 2 Hot Hors D'Oeuvres
· 1 Hot Pasta or Rice
· Choice of 2 Hot Entrees
· 1 Vegetable Dish
· Fresh Baked Bread and Rolls
$10.95 per person

All Buffets Subject to 20 Person Minimum

DELUXE HOT BUFFET
Choice of:
· 4 Hot Hors D'Oeuvres
· 2 Hot Pasta or Rice
· 3 Hot Entrees
· 1 Vegetable Dish
· Fresh Baked Bread and Rolls
$12.95 per person

HOT ITEMS

HOT ENTREES
CHICKEN CORDON BLEU
CHICKEN MARSALA
HAWAIIAN CHICKEN
BBQ CHICKEN
CHICKEN FRANCESE
CAJUN CHICKEN
CHICKEN AND BROCCOLI
CHICKEN CUTLET PARMIGIANA
ROAST TURKEY
BEEF AND BROCCOLI
STEAK PIZZAIOLA
STEAK TERIYAKI
PEPPER STEAK
SWEDISH MEATBALLS
SAUSAGE AND PEPPERS
BBQ RIBS
BAKED VIRGINIA HAM
EGGPLANT PARMIGIANA
SALMON ALFREDO
LINGUINI WITH SHRIMP
FILLET OF SOLE FRANCESE
SEAFOOD MARINARA

VEGETABLE DISHES
BROCCOLI OREGANATO
ROASTED POTATOES
BABY CARROTS
STRING BEANS ALMONDINE
STEAMED VEGETABLE MEDLEY

HOT PASTA OR RICE
RICE PILAF
ORIENTAL FRIED RICE
PASTA PRIMAVERA
STUFFED SHELLS
BAKED ZITI
LINGUINI MARINARA
MANICOTTI
TORTELLINI IN RED SAUCE
LINGUINI WITH CLAM SAUCE

HORS D'OEUVRES
POTATO PUFFS
SPINACH PUFFS
MINI QUICHE LORRAINE
FRANKS IN A BLANKET
STUFFED MUSHROOMS
MINI DEEP DISH PIZZA
SWEDISH MEATBALLS
POTATO PANCAKES
CHEESE PUFFS
MINI EGG ROLLS
SPARE RIBS
SPINACH QUICHE
BAKED CLAMS
MINI KNISHES
CHICKEN WINGS
STUFFED POTATO SKINS
MOZZARELLA STICKS
CHICKEN TENDERS

All Hot Buffets are Served in Attractive Aluminum Trays with
Chafing Stands and Sterno Heat. Plastic Service Includes Heavy Forks,
Knives, Dinner Plates, Napkins, Serving Utensils, and Cocktail Toothpicks.
Delivered and Set Up Ready to Serve on Your Table.

PARTY HEROS
Layer Upon Layer of Our Delicious Boars Head Cold Cuts
ITALIAN STYLE
Genoa Salami, Ham, Pepperoni, Provolone, Mozzarella,
Lettuce, Tomato, Oil and Vinegar
AMERICAN STYLE
Fresh Roast Beef, Turkey Breast, Virginia Ham,
Swiss Cheese, American Cheese, Lettuce, Tomatoes,
Mustard and Mayonnaise

3 FEET - $35.00 (12-15 people)
4 FEET - $45.00 (15-20 people)
5 FEET - $55.00 (20-25 people)
6 FEET - $65.00 (25-30 people)

SPECIALTY PLATTERS

ASSORTED HOT HORS D'OEUVRES
Choice of Any 4 Items on Our List (Serves 20-25 People) $39.00

FRESH VEGETABLE PLATTER
An Assortment of Garden Fresh Raw Vegetables with a
Delicious Dip. (Serves 15-20 People) $29.00

INTERNATIONAL CHEESE PLATTER
A Fine Selection of Imported and Domestic Cheeses, Decoratively
Arranged and Garnished. (Serves 15-20 People) $39.00

SHRIMP COCKTAIL PLATTER
Jumbo Shrimp Arranged on a Bed of Lettuce, Served with Cocktail
Sauce and Garnished with Lemon Wedges. (Serves 15-20 People) $39.00

FINGER SANDWICH PLATTER
Triple Layer Sandwiches with Roast Beef, Turkey, Virginia Ham,
and American Cheese. Garnished with Olives and Pickles.
(Serves 15-20 People) $29.00

BUFFALO WING PLATTER
Hot and Spicy Chicken Wings Served with Bleu Cheese Dressing
and Celery Sticks. (Serves 15-20 People) $29.00

FRESH FRUIT PLATTER
A Colorful Assortment of Fresh Fruit, Subject to Seasonal
Availability. $29.00

paper stock
80# Cover Cougar

typeface
Arial by ProGraphics

printing technique
Offset Lithography

number of color inks
Four-color Process

number produced
1,000

design budget
$5,000

111

restaurant
Elka Definitive Seafood

location
San Francisco, California

design firm
Group 425

designer/copywriter
Linda Stroman

illustrator
Brett Kladney

year produced
1992

CONCEPT

Printed on vellum and affixed to Japanese paper, the menu design for Elka Definitive Seafood lends subtle allusions to fish.

SPECIAL VISUAL EFFECTS

Each bold letter of Elka's logo is illustrated with underwater images.

TRENDS FOR THE '90s

"Simple, practical, new 'plastic papers' for covers. Imprinting actual menu off laser printer."

paper stock
Strathmore, Vellum

typeface
Helvetica *(slightly modified)*

printing technique
Five-color over solid with reverse Embossed

number of color inks
Five

number produced
2,000 of each

design budget
$5,000

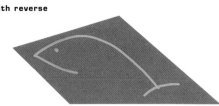

restaurant
Amapola
(Hotel Principe Felipe)

location
La Manga, Spain

design firm
David Carter Design

designer/illustrator
Lori Wilson

copywriter
Hotel Principe Felipe

year produced
1993

CONCEPT

Amapola is a casual al fresco cafe named after the Spanish word for poppy. These beautiful native flowers surround the property of the Hotel Principe Felipe in Spain. A stylized representation of the poppy appears on the menu covers, accented by a bold stripe pattern.

paper stock
Simpson Starwhite Vicksburg

typefaces
Tiffany Demi, Futura

printing technique
Offset Lithography

number of color inks
Four PMS

number produced
500

restaurant
La Samanna *(Rosewood Hotels, Dallas, Texas)*

location
St. Martin, French West Indies

design firm
David Carter Design

designer
Sharon LeJeune

illustrator
found art

year produced
1992

CONCEPT

La Samanna's menu highlights their sea-side location and fresh seafood through a color scheme and pattern that bring to mind waves crashing on the shore of a sandy beach. The menus are flexible, as new pages can be easily inserted.

paper stock
Simpson Quest, Evergreen

printing technique
Offset Lithography

number of color inks
Two PMS

number produced
1,500

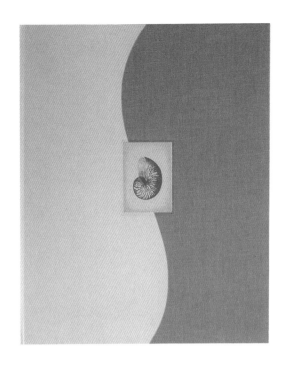

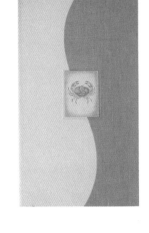

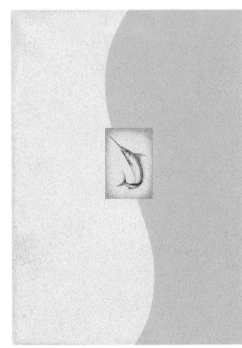

restaurant
Snappers Seafood Restaurant

location
Savannah, Georgia

design firm
The Menu Workshop

designer
Liz Kearney

copywriters
Snappers Seafood Restaurant
The Menu Workshop

year produced
1993

CONCEPT

Snappers Seafood Restaurant's new menu uses extensive color and develops a variety of sections with unique heading treatments. Illustrations further enhance their seafood image.

For greater merchandising, lunch and dinner sections were created on the menu, resulting in increased sales for each day. A fair amount of descriptive copy was also added, and the actual placement of the items was reworked.

paper stock
French Speckletone

typefaces
Bodoni, Stone

printing technique
Offset Lithography

number of color inks
Three

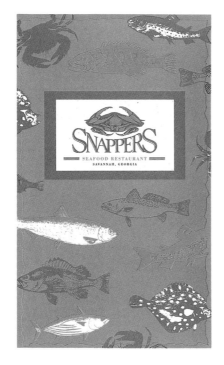

SEATTLE COMMERCIAL PHOTOWORKS

restaurant
Snaps

location
New York, New York

design firm
Monica Banks & Company

designer/illustrator
Monica Banks

copywriters
Hakan Swahn *(Menus)*
Monica Banks *(Holiday Card)*

year produced
1992

CONCEPT

Snaps serves Scandinavian cuisine and wants to be known for its fish dishes. The logo, representing two fish swimming to form an *S*, was composed primarily in yellow and blue, the colors of the Swedish flag. The name of the restaurant is slang for the Scandinavian drink aquavit (the name of Snaps's sister restaurant, which is more formal). The logo, and the free swim depicted on the menu and wine list covers, plates, and holiday card are meant to evoke the sensuousness and whimsy of the restaurant's interior and food.

paper stock
15pt Carolina Coated Tag

typefaces
Columna *(logo)*
Cochin Bold Roman and Italic

printing technique
Offset *(menu covers)*
Photocopy *(inserts)*

number produced
2,000

230 Park Avenue
At 46th Street
New York NY 10169
Tel. (212) 949-7878

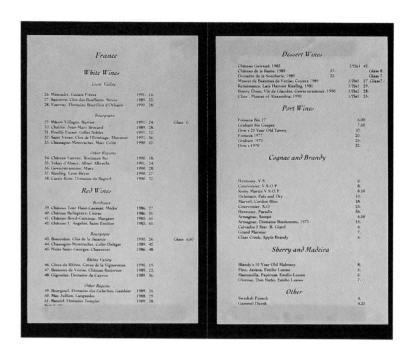

restaurant
Café Nola

location
Philadelphia, Pennsylvania

design firm
Amalgamation House, Inc.

designers
Diane Zatz
Judith De Vicaris
Bill Curry

illustrator
Diane Zatz

copywriter
Judith De Vicaris

year produced
1992

CONCEPT

Café Nola was a New Orleans style restaurant until the addition of two new rooms expanded its menu to include foods from Florida and the Islands. The colorful map approach provides a way to convey this expanded range of cuisine to patrons. A horizontal format offered the restaurateurs a chance to better organize their selection. Seasonal specials are featured separately from the regular appetizers and entrées. Pre-printed category pages allow the restaurant to change their specials more often without reprinting the whole menu.

JUDITH DE VICARIS

JUDITH DE VICARIS
CUISINE OF NEW ORLEANS

Café Nola

— that's NO for New Orleans and LA for Louisiana —
was founded a dozen years ago just before the Paul Prudhomme Cajun craze swept the country.

Proprietors Judy DeVicaris and Bill Curry thought that
the cuisine and fun atmosphere of New Orleans were a perfect match for South Street,
Philadelphia's entertainment and night life district.
"We wanted a great cuisine that could be enjoyed without being pretentious."

Because of its great success,
Café Nola has added two dining rooms and a second bar during the ensuing years.
The restaurant has also expanded its culinary horizons
by adding the Creole food of the Caribbean to its New Orleans repertoire.
The present menu cover by Diane Zatz reflects the restaurant's tropical culinary world.

Although the main thrust of Nola's menu is Creole (the refined, haute cuisine of the city),
there is an abundance of Cajun specialties featuring French Acadian rustic touches.
Under the tutelage of Terry Thompson, noted author and authority on the culinary history of New Orleans,
we have created a menu of truly authentic dishes faithful to this dual heritage.

The menu has also been influenced by contributions from the famous Book and the Cook authors
who have been our guests over the years.*
You'll even find a touch of the Orient in our delicious nightly specials!

Although many of the foods are spicy, Nola's menu has many dishes without the "fiery fun of peppers".
If you are on a restricted diet, just tell your waitperson and our chef
will happily create a delicious dish within those restrictions.
The Chef also welcomes vegetarian requests.

Please refrain from cigar, clove cigarette or pipe smoking.

Book and the Cook guests chefs: **Terry Thompson, author of "Cajun and Creole Cooking"; PBS stars **Natalie Dupree** and*
***Jeff Smith** ("The Frugal Gourmet"); **John Folse**, of the restaurant "Lafite's Landing"; **Norman VanAiken**, author of "Feast of Sunlight";*
***Hugh Carpenter**, author of "Pacific Flavors" and "Chopstix"; **Linda Gassheimer**, columnist of the Miami Herald, and author of*
*"Keys Cuisine"; and **Kevin Graham**, executive chef at the Windsor Court Hotel in New Orleans and the author of "Simply Elegant".*

WINES BY THE GLASS

SPARKLING WINES

Freixenet Carta Nevada	4.00
Piper Sonoma	6.50

WHITE WINES

Pouilly Fume, *Les Chantalouettes*	7.50
Chardonnay, *Groth*	7.00
Chardonnay, *Sterling*	6.00
Chardonnay, *Gallo*	4.00
Graves, *Chateau Magneau*	5.50
Gewurztraminer, *Gundlach Bundschu*	4.50
Sauvignon Blanc, *Jacob's Creek*	4.50
White Zinfandel, *Sutter Home*	4.00
White Zinfandel, *Gallo*	3.50

RED WINES

Cabernet, *William Hill Silver Label*	5.75
Cabernet, *Woodbridge*	
Robert Mondavi	4.25
Merlot, *Columbia Crest*	4.75
Medoc, *Chateau Greysac*	4.50
Charbono, *Inglenook*	5.25
Beaujolais, *Chateau de La Chaize*	4.75
Bordeaux, *Mouton Cadet*	4.75

BOTTLED WATERS

Ty-nant, sparkling	2.50
Evian, still	2.50

WINES BY THE GLASS

COCKTAILS

COLD APPETIZERS

HOT APPETIZERS

SEASONAL SPECIALS

ENTRÉES

TRENDS FOR THE '90s

"Menu design in the nineties will be less gimmicky and more informational. We have always chosen to be descriptive in our menus and have gradually drifted from 'clever' names to more information on foods. We still try to offer both, but we feel we need to educate our customers on new menu items. We also feel spoken specials can be minimized by our use of changing specials selection."

paper stock
Laminated 3ml Clear on 65# Vellum

typeface
Times Roman *(cover, inserts)*

printing technique
"Rapidocolor" *(cover)*
Offset Lithography *(inserts)*

number of color inks
Four-color *(cover)*

number produced
1,000

design budget
under $1,000

restaurant
Hemingways *(The Hyatt Grand Cayman)*

location
Grand Cayman

design firm
Associates Design

art director
Charles Polonsky

designer
Beth Finn

illustrator
Local Artist from Grand Cayman

CONCEPT

Hemingways supplied three native lithographs for use in the design of its menus. The unique style, exhibited in each graphic, not only represents the restaurant's seafood theme but also its tropical location. Incorporated into a handwritten logo, textures and colors from the lithographs were applied to the menus. Each logo distinguishes between lunch, dinner and dessert. Ribbon corners bind the one-color master laser sheets.

paper stock
Buckskin® by Kimberley Clark

typeface
Hand Script

printing technique
Offset Lithography

number of color inks
Four-color Process *(cover)*
One *(inside)*

number produced
750 of each

restaurant
Gus' Place

location
New York, New York

design firm
PM Design & Marketing

designer/illustrator
Philip Marzo

copywriter
Anna Herman

year produced
1992

CONCEPT

Recently renovated with a new cuisine, Gus' Place's main concern was how to win over established clientele and attract new customers. The new interior architecture dictated the direction of the graphics program. Walls of large, open double doors created an airy, cafe feel. The cut-paper graphics tie in this open-air atmosphere with classic Greek icons such as fish, the fig and the sea. The choice of blue ink and parchment stock suggest the Mediterranean Sea and sky. Architecture and graphics work well to announce the restaurant's new direction.

paper stock
Parchment

typeface
Kabel

number of color inks
One

number produced
500

design budget
Under $3,000

Pikilia & Antipasto

A Selection of Roasted, Grilled Marinated Vegetables and Olives
small...$5.00   large...$8.00

Small Plates and Salads

Basket of Tiny Fried Fish...$5.00
Fried Calamari with Anchovy Toasts and Tomato Relish...$5.50
Grilled Pepper and Eggplant Terrine with Sheep Cheese...$5.00
Three Greek Spreads served with Chili Potato Chips...$4.00
Rosemary Grilled Shellfish with Preserved Lemon...$6.50
Salt Cod Fritters with Skordalia (garlic almond mayonnaise)...$5.00
Grilled Stuffed Quail wrapped in Grape Leaves...$7.00

Mixed Green Salad with Fresh Herb Vinaigrette...$4.00
Salad of Fennel, Beet and Toasted Walnuts with Tarragon Vinaigrette...$5.00
Classic Greek Salad...$6.00

Breads & Savory Pastries

Crostini with House Smoked Tuna, Roast Pepper and Green Olive Puree...$6.00
Shredded Duck and Roquefort Calzone...$6.50
Three Phyllo Pastries - Spinach, Cheese, Lamb Sausage...$5.50
Pissaladiere - Tomato, Onion and Olive Pizza...$4.00

Large Plates

Whole Wheat Paparadelle with Greens, Pine Nuts and Pecorino Romano...$11.00
Linguini with Littleneck Clams, Garlic and Herb Oil...$11.50
Mediterranean Vegetable Plate...$10.50
Bourride - Provençal Fish Stew with Aioli and Croutons...$15.50
Baked Shrimp in Spicy Tomato Sauce with Feta Cheese...$13.50
Fish of the Day - Choice of Sauce: Charred Tomato, Ladolemono, Herb Vinaigrette...Priced Below
Grilled Tuna with White Bean, Cilantro and Seville Orange...$15.50
Roast Duck with Mint and Wild Greens served with Red Lentils...$14.50
Roast Chicken Stuffed with Fresh Bay Leaves and Roast Garlic...$12.50
Traditional Lamb Souvlaki with Tzatziki...$15.50
Braised Lamb Shanks with Fragrant Couscous...$14.50

Soup of the Day

Side Plates - $3.50

Grilled Fennel

Fragrant Couscous

Ratatouille in Polenta Crust

Herb Roasted Potatoes

Wilted Greens

Tzatziki - Cucumber Yogurt Salad
with Mint

Grilled Vegetable Brochette

Desserts - $6.50

Honey & Bitter Orange Crème Brûlée

Saffron Rice Pudding

Chocolate Blackberry Mousse Cake

Homemade Ice Creams and Sorbets

Lemon Poppy Seed Tartlette

Figs Poached in Port with Mascarpone

Country Cheese Plate

Gus' Place
MEDITERRANEAN CAFE & BAR

Private Dining Room
Available -
Up to 35 Guests.
Call 212.645.8511

Gus' Place
MEDITERRANEAN CAFE & BAR

Stop in and enjoy the open door, summer breezes
at the new Gus' Place.
Fresh and fragrant flavors from the seaside towns
bordering the Mediterranean Sea.

Specialties include:
Tzatziki - Cucumber Yogurt Salad with Mint...$3.50

Greek Antipasto...$5.00

Fried Calamari with Anchovy Toasts and Tomato Relish...$5.50

Rosemary Grilled Shellfish with Preserved Lemon...$6.50

Three Phyllo Pastries - Spinach, Cheese, Lamb Sausage...$5.50

Pissaladiere - Tomato, Onion and Olive Pizza...$4.00

Linguini with Littleneck Clams, Garlic and Herb Oil...$11.50

Grilled Tuna with White Bean, Cilantro and Seville Orange...$15.50

Traditional Lamb Souvlaki with Tzatziki...$15.50

Lunch   Dinner   Late Night   Sunday Brunch   Seven Days
Private Parties

149 Waverly Place - Just West of 6th Avenue -
Greenwich Village, NYC 10014 - Tel. 212.645.8511

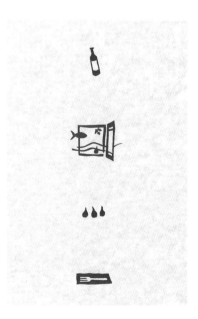

restaurants
The Crab Pot and North Beach Deli

location
San Francisco International Airport, California

design firm
JRDC

art director
Judi Radice Hays

designer
Kathy Warinner

illustrator
Rik Olson *(Crab Pot)*

year produced
1993

CONCEPT

The idea for the suitcase cover design was derived from vestiges of "the golden era of travel" when every trip was an adventure, and certainly a San Francisco destination was as alluring then as it is now. The design team fashioned the contents of the menu after the regions that created the fare presented in the restaurant. Travel stickers, icons of each restaurant's identity, were created and hand-applied to the menu covers. The menu pages are inserted and tied in place with colored jute.

paper stock
Buckskin® by Kimberley Clark *(cover)*
Strathmore Natural *(inserts)*

printing technique
Offset Lithography

number of color inks
Four-color Process *(stickers)*
One PMS *(cover)*

number produced
2,000

122

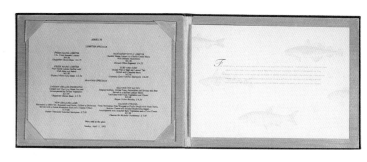

KLEIN & WILSON PHOTOGRAPHY

CHILDREN'S DINNER MENU
Ariel the Little Mermaid asked her seagull friend Scuttle to tell her the names of
our delicious food! Scuttle always says he's an expert at these things!

GUPSNARES AND GO-ZACKEES
Fish & Chips (Fresh Batter Dipped) 5.50

DINGLEHOPPER'S DELIGHT
Spaghetti and Meat Sauce 3.95

GOLDEN GAGGLESMACKERS
Fresh Chicken Nuggets 4.25

restaurant
Ariel's

location
**Walt Disney World,
Lake Buena Vista, Florida**

design firm
David Carter Design

art director
David Carter

designer
Randall Hill

illustrator
Glen Davis

copywriter
Ariel's

year produced
1991

CONCEPT

Ariel's is an underwater fantasy restaurant at Disney's Beach Club Resort. The menu design reflects this theme in a subtly sophisticated manner.

SPECIAL VISUAL EFFECTS

Soft metallic colors were used to create a "shimmering" quality like one might experience underwater.

paper stock
Simpson Starwhite Vicksburg

typeface
Garamond

printing technique
Four-color Process, Metallic Ink

number of color inks
Six, Varnish on covers

number produced
1,000

6

Unusual

restaurant
Stacks'

location
Burlingame, California

design firm
Bruce Yelaska Design

designer/illustrator
Bruce Yelaska

year produced
1993

CONCEPT

Stacks' was named and designed to express and emphasize the idea of a large traditional American breakfast. *Stacks* is a common restaurant term used to describe the amount of pancakes in an order. By making the last *s* in Stacks' possessive it looks as if the chef's name is also Stacks. The logo shows the chef holding a bounty of pancakes proudly in his arms. The stack is so high, it nearly obscures him.

SPECIAL VISUAL EFFECTS

The stacking idea is continuously played upon. The business cards are scored, so when folded, the name, address and phone number all stack on top of each other. This scoring also allows the cards to stand up like displays or table tents, and makes them a whimsical take-away item. Menus stand up on set tables signaling that the tables are ready for customers.

paper stock
Champion Benefit, French Speckletone

typefaces
Futura Bold Condensed, Gill Sans

printing technique
Offset Lithography

number of color inks
Two PMS

number produced
1,000

design budget
$10,000

STACKS'

TOM DUFFY

361 CALIFORNIA DR.

BURLINGAME, CA 94103

415.579.1384

STACKS'

BREAKFAST
&
LUNCH

BREAKFAST BASICS
Two eggs, potatoes and bagel
2.95
Bacon, two eggs, potatoes and bagel
4.75
Pork sausage, two eggs and bagel
4.75
Ham, two eggs,potatoes and bagel
4.75
Chicken apple sausage, two eggs, potatoes and bagel
4.95

CREPES
Homemade sweet crepes, with whipped eggs, served with potatoes and bagel
GARDEN CREPE
Avocado, mushrooms, onions, bell pepper, jack cheese, tomato, sour cream and chives
4.95
FRUIT CREPE
Seasonal fresh fruit topped with low fat yogurt
4.95
CRAB CREPE
Fresh crab meat, chives and avocado, topped with hollandaise sauce
6.25
MIGHTY MEAT CREPES
Ham, bacon, sausage, onion, onion mushroom, avocado, cheddar-jack cheese, sour cream and chives
6.25

THREE EGG SCRAMBLES
All scrambles topped with cheddar-jack cheese and served with potatoes and bagel
Hot links, green chili, onions, mushrooms, with salsa on the side
5.75
Mushrooms, onions, broccoli, celery, zucchini and diced tomato
5.50
Chorizo, green chili, onions, black olives, guacamole and sour cream with salsa on the side
5.95
Bacon, mushroom and spinach
5.50

SKILLETS
Our great potatoes topped with cheddar-jack cheese, your choice of two eggs and bagel
5.75
FRESH VEGETABLES
BACON AND ONIONS
HOT LINKS,MUSHROOMS AND ONIONS
GREEN CHILI, ONIONS AND SALSA
HAM AND MUSHROOMS
SAUSAGE AND MUSHROOMS

FRITTATAS
Three whipped eggs cooked open face, topped with cheddar-jack cheese, served with potatoes and bagel
CRAB FRITTATAS
Crab meat, onions, avocado, tomato, with hollandaise on the side
6.95
HAM FRITTATAS
Diced ham, onions, black olives, topped with swiss cheese, sour cream and chives
5.95
MEXICAN FRITTATAS
Chorizo, onion, green chili, tomatoes, salsa, sour cream, chives and guacamole
6.75
VEGETARIAN FRITTATAS
Diced fresh vegetables, salsa, sour cream and chives
5.95

STACKS' HOUSE SPECIALS
STEAK AND EGGS
Broiled 5oz. top sirloin, choice of two eggs, potatoes and bagel
7.50
EGGS BENEDICT
Two poached eggs, ham and spinach on an english muffin topped with hollandaise
6.95
EGGS FLORENTINE
Two poached eggs, ham and spinach on an english muffin topped with hollandaise
6.95
EGGS LOUIS
Two poached eggs, crab meat and spinach on an english muffin, topped with hollandaise
7.50

OUR SUPER OMELETS
Served with potatoes and bagel
VEGGIE
Fresh diced vegetables, cheddar-jack cheese, sour cream and chives
5.25
WEST
Ham, bell pepper,onion and cheddar-jack cheese
5.50
MEXICAN
Chorizo, avocado, green chili, onions, salsa, cheddar-jack cheese,sour cream and chives
6.95
ALL MEAT
Ham, bacon, sausage, mushrooms, onions, diced tomatoes, sour cream and chives with salsa on the side
6.95
HOT LINKS
Diced hot links, green chili, onions, mushrooms, cheddar-jack cheese, sour cream and chives with salsa on the side
6.75
All American Favorites
Plain Omelet
3.75
Cheese Omelet
4.50
Bacon and Cheese
4.95
Ham and Cheese
4.95
Sausage and Cheese
4.95
Mushroom and Cheese
6.75

Stacks' Homemade Pancakes
Full stack (5) Also available short stack (3) and single
Plain
3.25
Blueberry
4.75
Blue Germ
4.95
Banana wheat germ
4.95
Raisin Walnut
4.75
Wheat Germ
4.25

OLD FASHIONED BELGIUM WAFFLES
PLAIN WAFFLE
4.25
APPLE WAFFLE
Topped with apples in a cinnamon glaze with fresh whipped cream
4.75
BLUEBERRY WAFFLE
Blueberries in a blueberry glaze and fresh whipped cream
4.75
STRAWBERRY WAFFLE
(In season) with fresh whipped cream
4.75
BANANA-PECAN WAFFLE
Topped with roasted Georgian pecans, sliced bananas and fresh whipped cream
4.95
BACON WAFFLE
With bits of real diced bacon
4.95

FRENCH TOAST
Three thick slices of Texas toast dipped in a vanilla, cream and cinnamon egg batter
4.25

BEVERAGES
ESPRESSO 1.25
CAPPUCCINO 1.75
CAFE LATTE 1.95
HOT CHOCOLATE WITH WHIPPED CREAM 1.50
COFFEE / DECAF .90
TEA .90
FRESH SQUEEZED ORANGE JUICE 1.50
FRESH SQUEEZED GRAPEFRUIT JUICE 1.50
TOMATO JUICE 1.50
UNFILTERED APPLE JUICE 1.50
CRANBERRY JUICE 1.50

SIDE ORDERS
POTATOES 1.75
TOAST 1.00
SAUSAGE 2.25
CHICKEN APPLE SAUSAGE 2.95
BACON 2.25
HAM 1.95
BAGEL 1.25
CREAM CHEESE .75

restaurant
Finalè Dessert Cafe

location
Indianapolis, Indiana

design firm
Stahl Design, Inc.

designer
David Stahl

copywriter
Dennis Collins

year produced
1993

CONCEPT

Each menu has an actual dessert fork attached to the top in the formal place-set position. The fork serves as a symbol for the only food on the menu—desserts. Its importance is heightened by the lack of any word or other visual on the cover. The fork also serves as a binder for the loose-leaf pages of the menu itself.

Dessert poetry—to get you in the mood and rid you of any guilt—is featured with the logo and a short verse from the Beatles song *Savoy Truffle* on the second page of the cover.

SPECIAL VISUAL EFFECTS

The forks are all different, and are flattened so they are easily stackable and less prone to injure.

TRENDS FOR THE '90s

"More cost-effective, environment-conscious. More conceptual ideas. New materials and binding methods."

paper stock
Fox River Confetti

typefaces
Burlington, Gill Sans

printing technique
Offset Lithography

number of color inks
Two, Three

number produced
250

design budget
$2,500

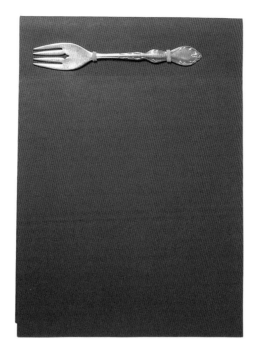

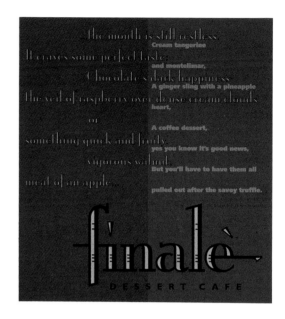

restaurant
Zoë

location
New York, New York

design firm
John Kneapler Design

designer
John Kneapler

year produced
1992

CONCEPT

Zoë is named for the grandmother of one of the owners, and the design expresses the grandmother's originality and "free-spirit," while keeping the semblance of a specific ethnicity vague. To avoid the ever-present block letters used by galleries and retail stores throughout the Soho neighborhood, the logo was customized into a "Zoë Alphabet." Menus are printed in-house and slipped into clear, plastic sheaths with no border flaps.

SPECIAL VISUAL EFFECTS

The menu's copper foil stamping enhances the building's exterior copper cornice and presence as a landmark. The copper foil stamping adds a visual warmth to the exterior.

paper stock
80# Curtis Tuscan Terra

typeface
Calligraphy

printing technique
Hot-stamped, Copper Foil

number of color inks
Two

number produced
4,000

design budget
$2,500

DESSERTS

Valrhona Chocolate Pudding Cake
with Gianduja Ice Cream
$7.00

Warm Apple Cranberry Crisp
with Chinese Five-Spice Ice Cream
$6.00

Caramelized Banana and Walnut Tart
with Creme Fraiche
$7.00

Brown Butter Pear Tart with Cinnamon Ice Cream
& Caramel Sauce
$6.00

Marinated Strawberries with Orange Biscuits
& Brandied Whipped Cream
$7.00

Assortment of House Made
Ice Creams or Sorbets
$5.00

Assorted Fresh Fruit and Berries.
$8.00

Pastry Chef: Cristina Echiverri

SUNDAYS
BRUNCH 12-3 PM
MAGNUM DINNERS 5-10 PM

SPECIALLY SELECTED MAGNUMS
OF AMERICA'S BEST WINES,
RATED BY THE *WINE SPECTATOR*,
WILL BE SERVED BY THE GLASS

90 PRINCE STREET

GRILL • ROTISSERIE • BRICK OVEN
LUNCH • DINNER • WEEKEND BRUNCH
CLOSED MONDAYS

RESERVATIONS (212) 966-6722

PHOTOGRAPHY COURTESY OF ZOË

128

restaurant
Anzu Restaurant

location
Dallas, Texas

design firm
David Carter Design

designer
Sharon LeJeune

year produced
1993

CONCEPT

The design team has created a unique menu that echoes the restaurant's natural Japanese cuisine.

SPECIAL VISUAL EFFECTS

Hand-stamped logo, handmade paper, and natural stick binding.

TRENDS FOR THE '90s

"...Unusually textured handmade papers and more unique approaches to materials...combine for a more artful, personal and handmade approach to menu design."

paper stock
Simpson Quest, Handmade Cover

typeface
Futura

printing technique
Laser-printed Inserts

number produced
250

restaurant
Plaza San Antonio Hotel *(Sun & Moon Menu)*

location
San Antonio, Texas

design firm
Martelle Design

designer
Carol Martelle Potter

illustrator/copywriter
Carol Martelle Potter

year produced
1993

CONCEPT

In San Antonio, the summer days are warm, sunny and soothing. At night, there are often warm southerly breezes and beautiful skies. The designer's goal was to capture both of these in this menu.

SPECIAL VISUAL EFFECTS

This menu takes advantage of the qualities of corrugated plastic: the colors on one side interact with the menu on the other, but the menu still performs its primary function, to tell people what they can order.

paper stock
Corrugated Plastic

typefaces
Univers, Charlemagne

printing technique
Screen Printing

number of color inks
Two

number produced
150

design budget
$1,500

ROBERT FRENCH

ROBERT FRENCH

ROBERT FRENCH

ROBERT FRENCH

restaurant
Plaza San Antonio Hotel *(Pool Menu)*

location
San Antonio, Texas

design firm
Meridian 28 Design

art director
Ginny Garcia

illustrators
Robert French
James B. Donegan

copywriters
Ginny Garcia
James B. Donegan

year produced
1993

CONCEPT

The designers considered poolside activities such as mask painting and papier-mâché when developing the design concept. They developed a system of menus that resemble pre-Columbian masks, both interactive with each other and the restaurant's patrons. The menus are interlocking and can be connected to make a sculpture.

SPECIAL VISUAL EFFECTS

While sitting poolside, one can see the graphics on one side through the light. The menus are also waterproof and able to withstand the elements of nature.

paper stock
Corrugated Plastic

typefaces
Lithos, Follies

printing technique
Screen Printing

number of color inks
Three

number produced
50

design budget
$1,500

ROBERT FRENCH

ROBERT FRENCH

restaurant
Kotobuki Restaurant

location
Stamford, Connecticut

design firm
Erica Ando Design

designer
Erica Ando

year produced
1990

CONCEPT

The wait staff at Kotobuki Restaurant
become walking menus in these T-shirts.
The T-shirts are also sold at the restaurant,
creating walking advertisements outside.

TRENDS FOR THE '90s
"Paper menus will be obsolete."

typeface
Helvetica

printing technique
Heat Transfer

number of color inks
One

number produced
Over 300

restaurant
The Simon House

location
Milwaukee, Wisconsin

design firm
Becker Design

designer
Neil Becker

year produced
1993

CONCEPT

This menu was designed for an upscale restaurant in existence for more than 50 years. A new logo was created and the elongated *S* was used to create a unique and interesting shape.

SPECIAL VISUAL EFFECTS

The die-cut *S* is easily recognized when the menu is closed, due to the contrast in color of the duplex stock. When the menu is open, the type follows the line of the then reversed *S* shape.

paper stock
Neenah Duplex Stock

typefaces
Helvetica Condensed, Bodoni

printing technique
Offset Lithography

number of color inks
Three

number produced
300

design budget
$4,000

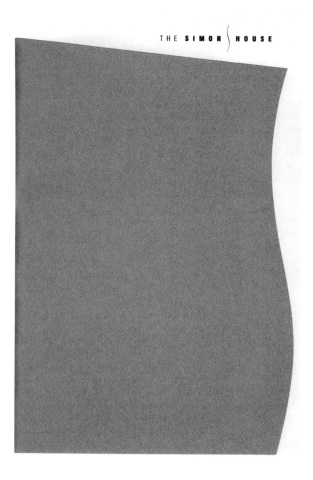

THE SIMON ❯ HOUSE

THE SIMON ❯ HOUSE

APPETIZERS

Homemade Soup du Jour — 1.50
Made fresh daily.

Onion Rings — 3.95
Freshly shredded Bermudas - lightly breaded and piled high.

Mozerella Marinara — 4.50
5 sticks of Wisconsin's finest. Served with our tangy marinara sauce.

Fresh Blue Points — 4.95
Premium oysters on the half-shell.

Oysters Rockefeller — 6.95
Blue Points topped with spinach and onion, baked and served with a hollandaise sauce.

Chili con Carne — 2.75
Served in a cup, topped with cheddar cheese.

Jumbo Shrimp Cocktail — 6.95
5 large shrimp served with cocktail sauce.

Crab Rangoon — 4.95
Deep fried pastry stuffed with crab & cream cheese.

Seafood Ravioli with Pesto Sauce — 5.25
Fisherman's choice.

Bronzed Shrimp and Scallop Brochette — 5.95
2 jumbo shrimp and 3 scallops grilled with tomato and onion then glazed with our seafood barbeque sauce.

Liver Paté — 3.25
Served with assorted crackers.

SALAD PANTRY

Chicken Caesar Salad — 8.25
Grilled marinated chicken breast strips served warm on a bed of fresh romaine.

Chef's Salad — 7.95
Julienne strips of cheddar and Swiss cheese, turkey breast and lean smoked ham. Served on a bed of greens.

Chicken Salad — 7.50
Chunks of boneless chicken tossed in a light dressing and served over a bed of lettuce.

Salmon Pasta Salad — 8.95
Fresh smoked salmon tossed with rotini pasta and our parmesan peppercorn dressing.

Seafood Salad — 10.95
Large shrimp, Alaskan king crab and Albacore tuna served on a mound of lettuce.

Crabmeat Avocado — 12.95
King crabmeat piled high on crisp lettuce and finished with sliced fresh avocado.

FROM THE DELI

All sandwiches are served with coleslaw, potato chips and dill pickle.

Roast Beef and Cheddar — 6.95
Thinly sliced roast sirloin piled on a fresh sour dough roll with aged cheddar, horseradish sauce, onion, lettuce and tomato. Served hot.

Philadelphia Cheese Steak — 8.25
Thinly sliced roast sirloin smothered in sauteed peppers, onions and mozzarella cheese. Served on a toasted French bun. Served hot.

Reuben — 6.95
Shaved corned beef piled high on dark rye with Swiss cheese, sauerkraut and Thousand Island dressing. Served hot.

Grilled Ham and Swiss — 5.95
Thinly-sliced smoked ham stacked high with Swiss cheese.

California Croissant — 8.95
Shrimp and scallops delicately tossed in dressing with a hint of dill. Topped with lettuce and avocado. Served cold.

Croissant — 7.95
Your choice of sliced ham, corned beef or turkey. Topped with lettuce, tomato and mayo. Served cold.

Jumbo Clubhouse — 5.50
Three slices of toast, sliced turkey, bacon, lettuce, tomato and mayo. Served cold.

LUNCHEON DAILY FEATURES

> *Ask your server about today's specials.*

Simon House Au Gratin — 5.50
Sliced turkey served on toast points and topped with mushrooms, sherry sauce and shredded cheddar cheese.

Manhattan Au Gratin — 6.00
Sliced turkey and lean ham served on toast points with mushrooms, sherry sauce and cheddar cheese.

LUNCHEON SPECIALTIES

Roughy Four Seasons — 9.95
Broiled orange roughy topped with sauteed green and red peppers, onions and mushrooms.

Fresh Whitefish — 7.95
Broiled to perfection. Served with tartar sauce.

Liver and Onions — 6.25
Sauteed calves' liver served with glazed onions and crisp bacon.

Pasta Primavera — 7.95
Sauteed vegetables tossed with parmesan cheese sauce and tri-color rotini.

Chicken Pot Pie — 5.75
Large chunks of boneless chicken breast simmered in our rich sauce with mixed vegetables and mushrooms. Topped with a fine pastry crust.

Barbequed Ribs — 8.50
A half rack of pork ribs topped with our tangy sauce.

HOT JUMBO SANDWICHES

Hot sandwiches are served with French fries and coleslaw.

King-Sized Hamburger — 5.50
Broiled just the way you like it. Served on a kaiser or whole wheat roll. Garnished with lettuce and tomato.

Pepper Chicken — 5.95
Broiled boneless chicken topped with pepper cheese. Served on a kaiser with mayo.

Chili n' Cheese — 5.95
Our homemade chili con carne served mild or hot with a grilled cheese sandwich.

Tenderloin Steak — 9.95
U.S. Choice broiled to perfection. Served with grilled onions on a kaiser.

Strip Loin Steak — 9.95
Broiled and served on toast points.

Barbeque Beef — 6.25
U.S. Prime cubed and simmered in a tangy barbeque sauce. Served on a kaiser.

Hot Turkey — 5.50
Sliced turkey served open-faced on white bread.

restaurant
Kenny Rogers Roasters

location
Dallas, Texas

design firm
The Baker Agency

designer/copywriter
Mikie Baker

illustrator/photographer
Jim Foster

year produced
1992

CONCEPT

Because of Kenny Rogers' association with music, the menu for his Roasters restaurant was designed to look like a compact disc. An insert was designed that can be easily customized to each of the individual franchise's needs.

SPECIAL VISUAL EFFECTS

Menus look like compact discs with menu items listed in the place of song titles.

paper stock
Chipboard Box

typeface
Bodoni

printing technique
CD Label Printing

number of color inks
Four

number produced
5,000

design budget
$12,500

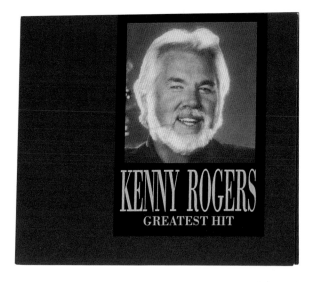

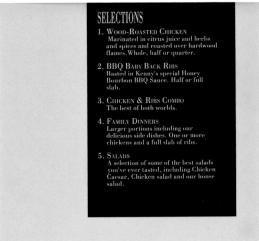

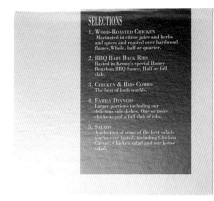

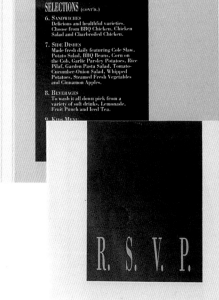

restaurant
Michael Jordan's, The Restaurant

location
Chicago, Illinois

design firm
Associates Design

art director/copywriter
Charles Polonsky

designers
Jill Arena
Donna Sommerville

illustrator
Roberta Serafini

year produced
1993

CONCEPT

Sports-bar themed Michael Jordan's, The Restaurant, presented a unique but understandable request in the design of its menus—keep it simple and inexpensive. The restaurant needed to have massive quantities of its menus on hand to keep pace with patrons and fans taking them as souvenirs. Also, because Michael Jordan's name and image are heavily copyrighted, the design had to move outside the realm of traditional Jordan symbolism.

The two-sided lunch and dinner menus meet desired goals, as the basic menu design unites the restaurant's logo art with the building's signage. The artwork on the children's menu is the winning illustration from a contest given by the *Chicago Tribune*.

SPECIAL VISUAL EFFECTS

The matching banquet folders are embossed to imitate the bumpy texture of a basketball.

typeface
Helvetica

printing technique
Offset Lithography

number of color inks
Two

number produced
5,000

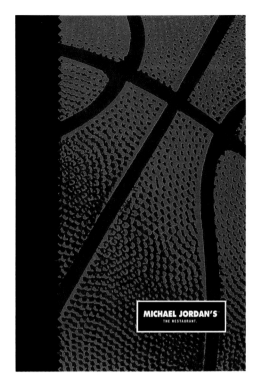

WINES BY THE GLASS

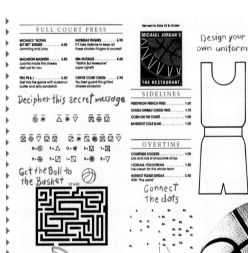

135

restaurant
Woods

location
**The Grand Hotel,
Mackinac Island, Michigan**

design firm
Reeser Advertising Associates

designer
Nancy Reeser

illustrators
Jeff Landis *(Dinner)*
Deborah Zapata *(Dessert)*

copywriter
Mimi Musser

year produced
1992

CONCEPT

Woods' menus work within the Bavarian theme of the restaurant. The dinner menu incorporates the wild flowers of Mackinac Island, and is decorated with a raffia ribbon. The dessert menu reflects a Bavarian cut-out paper motif. Both menus demonstrate the quality presentation of food in a fine dining atmosphere.

paper stock
Strathmore Americana *(Dinner)*
Astrolite *(Dessert)*

typeface
Media Graphics

printing technique
Offset Lithography

number of color inks
**Four-color Process
   + Two PMS** *(Dinner)*
Three PMS *(Dessert)*

number produced
500 each

design budget
$1,000 *(Dinner)*
$500 *(Dessert)*

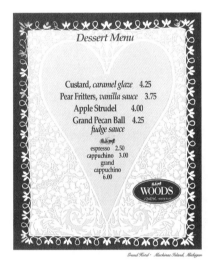

restaurant
The Jockey Club at the Grand Stand

location
**The Grand Hotel,
Mackinac Island, Michigan**

design firm
Reeser Advertising Associates

designer
Nancy Reeser

illustrator
Deborah Zapata

copywriter
Mimi Musser

year produced
1993

The Jockey Club
at the Grand Stand

CONCEPT

Both menus are designed to work within the equestrian theme of the Jockey Club restaurant. The dinner menu shows the restaurant's specially designed logo.

SPECIAL VISUAL EFFECTS

The dinner menu is designed to look like a horse's blanket. The lunch menu is die-cut to look lie a jockey's cap.

paper stock
15pt Carolina Cover

typeface
Media Graphics

printing technique
Offset Lithography

number of color inks
Three

number produced
600 *(Dinner)*
500 *(Lunch)*

design budget
$700 *(Dinner)*
$1,000 *(Lunch)*

restaurant
Wrigley Field *(Home of the Chicago Cubs: The*
Stadium Club, The Friendly Confines, The Sidewalk Cafe
and Mezzanine Box Catering)

location
Chicago, Illinois

design firm
The Levy Restaurants

creative director/designer
Marcy Lansing

illustrator
Marcy Lansing

year produced
1992

CONCEPT

The Stadium Club's menus are die-cut with
bright colors and look like tickets. Other
menus follow the baseball theme, as they
are all used in Wrigley Field.

paper stock
Champion Kromecote

typefaces
Helvetica, Brushscript

printing technique
Die-cut

number of color inks
Three PMS

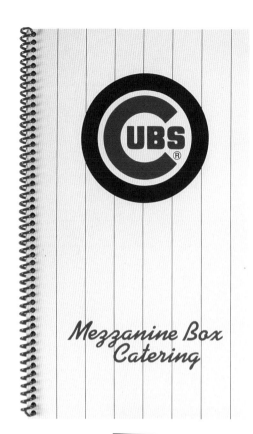

restaurant
Canopy's

location
Rochester, New York

design firm
D.A. Design

designer
Kathy D'Amanda

copywriter
Kevin Bedard

year produced
1988

CONCEPT

Canopy's restaurant actually has canopies over its tables. This led to the design of the menu, which is die-cut to look like a canopy.

paper stock
Strathmore Esprit White Cover

typefaces
Avant Garde *(body)*
Hand-drawn Art *(headers)*

printing technique
Bleeds, Scores, Die-cut

number of color inks
Two

number produced
2,000

design budget
$2,000

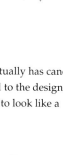

restaurant
Citrus of Boca

location
Boca Raton, Florida

designer
Andreas Reimann

copywriter
Graphic Dynamics *(Ft. Lauderdale)*

year produced
1992

CONCEPT
Cutting-edge, new-American, and very eclectic and artistic, this oversized menu reflects the cuisine offered at Citrus of Boca.

TRENDS FOR THE '90s
"Simple, explanatory, no hiding, price/ value relationship, readable, interesting in design, originality and reflecting overall concept."

paper stock
Recycled Stock

typeface
Handwritten

printing technique
Laser Copied *(color sprayed individually)*

number produced
200 *(menus)*
12 *(wine list covers)*

design budget
$3,000

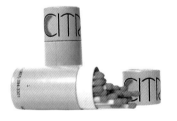

restaurant
Z Contemporary Cuisine

location
Woodmere Village, Ohio

design firm
Nesnadny and Schwartz

creative directors/designers
Joyce Nesnadny
Mark Schwartz

photographer
Tony Festa

copywriter
Zachary Bruell

CONCEPT

The client required a system of menus for a newly opened restaurant. The design system had to reflect the unique character of the physical space as well as the inventive nature of the offerings. At the same time, the entire system had to be engineered to accommodate daily updates to the menus.

The design team proposed a system of menu covers that utilized a relatively minimal design/color approach. The interiors employed a more vibrant color palette, as well as a pattern of photographic images of food. All of this was conceptually linked through the use of various graphic permutations of the letter Z.

paper stock
Various

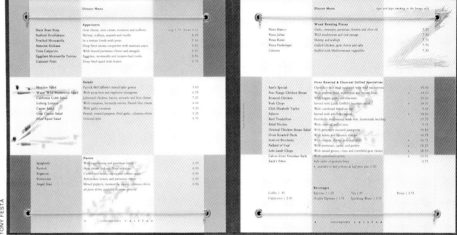

141

restaurant
Pete & Ernie's

location
New Stanton, Pennsylvania

design firm
Dragon's Teeth Design

designer
Gregory L. Hricenak

year produced
1993

CONCEPT

Pete & Ernie's decor looks like the reading room or study of an adventurer or world explorer. The diner is given a book which contains both lunch and dinner menus tipped into an actual hardbound book and marked with a bookmark (which doubles as a give-away). A third bookmark listing the day's specials may be inserted.

TRENDS FOR THE '90s

"The ability to economically change menu items and pricing is critical. However, the menu itself must not appear cheaply produced or quick copied. Novelty of design may often provide a means of bridging this gap."

paper stock
Couger Opaque *(menu)*
King James Royal *(bookmark)*

typeface
Bookman

printing technique
Offset Lithography

number of color inks
One

number produced
100 *(menus)*
500 *(bookmarks)*

design budget
$1,200 *(design, printing, assembly)*

restaurant
Hamburger Mary's

location
Seattle, Washington

design firm
Spangler Associates

designer
Ross Hogin

copywriter
Tracy Weir

CONCEPT

The Hamburger Mary's menu is reminiscent of the owners' "anything goes" hippie days.

The name is written in jumbled red and purple letters across the cover, and a stick and two green rubber bands cleverly hold the menu together. The inside is made of bright yellow pages which are scattered with bits of whimsical philosophy. Buckskin® was chosen for the menu cover because the restaurant wanted a durable, yet funky menu.

paper stock
Buckskin® by Kimberley Clark *(cover)*
Gilbert Esse *(inside)*

printing technique
Offset Lithography
PMS Color *(cover, inside)*
Opaque White Undercoat

number of color inks
Four *(cover)*
One *(inside)*

number produced
500

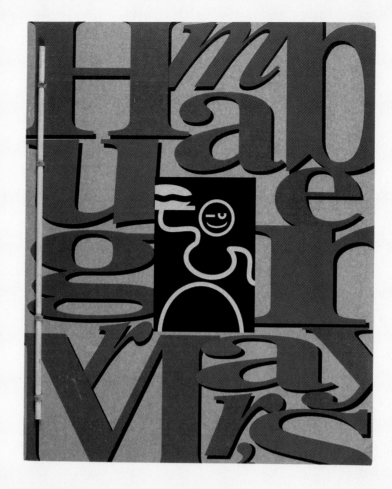

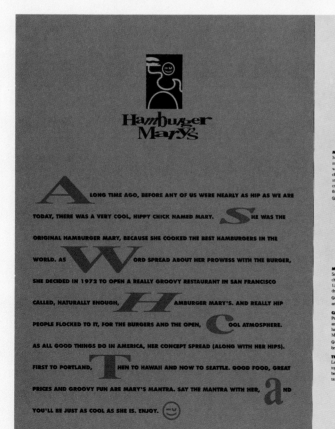

Hamburger Mary's

A LONG TIME AGO, BEFORE ANY OF US WERE NEARLY AS HIP AS WE ARE TODAY, THERE WAS A VERY COOL, HIPPY CHICK NAMED MARY. SHE WAS THE ORIGINAL HAMBURGER MARY, BECAUSE SHE COOKED THE BEST HAMBURGERS IN THE WORLD. AS WORD SPREAD ABOUT HER PROWESS WITH THE BURGER, SHE DECIDED IN 1972 TO OPEN A REALLY GROOVY RESTAURANT IN SAN FRANCISCO CALLED, NATURALLY ENOUGH, HAMBURGER MARY'S. AND REALLY HIP PEOPLE FLOCKED TO IT, FOR THE BURGERS AND THE OPEN, COOL ATMOSPHERE. AS ALL GOOD THINGS DO IN AMERICA, HER CONCEPT SPREAD (ALONG WITH HER HIPS). FIRST TO PORTLAND, THEN TO HAWAII AND NOW TO SEATTLE. GOOD FOOD, GREAT PRICES AND GROOVY FUN ARE MARY'S MANTRA. SAY THE MANTRA WITH HER, AND YOU'LL BE JUST AS COOL AS SHE IS. ENJOY.

Appetizers

MACHO NACHOS
Mucho nachos for the macho (or machoess?). A pile of chips topped with refried beans, olives, tomatoes, chicken taco meat and jalapeños, smothered with cheese. Vats of sour cream and our homemade salsa on the side. **$4.50**
☺ With guacamole **$5.50**

MARY'S MUSHROOMS
If only mushrooms had been like this in the '60s...Whole, sautéed with butter, spices and wine. **$4.95**
☺ Topped with melted Swiss Cheese **$5.95**

MARY'S WINGS
Buffalo's got nothing on Mary's red-hot chicken wings, served with celery sticks and bleu cheese dressing. Have six for **$3.95**
☺ Better yet, have ten for **$4.95**

MARY'S RIBS
Country-style, grilled with Mary's own molasses-laced BBQ sauce. A stack of napkins is waiting. **$5.95**

MARY'S STICKS
A new twist to satay — Mary's secret marinade makes them great. Mix or match three skewers of chicken or beef. **$4.95**

MARY'S FRIES
A huge basket of Mary's cross-cut fries (enough for two). **$2.50**
☺ Topped with a ton of cheese **$3.95**

MARY STRIPS
Tender filets of flash fried chicken breast with honey mustard dipping sauce. **$4.95**

SKINNY DIPPERS
Seasonal vegetables served with Mary's ranch dressing. **$4.95**

BAR FUEL
Chips with Mary's homemade salsa. **$2.95**

MARY'S MIX
Seasonal mixed greens with a choice of herbal vinaigrette, ranch, 1,000 island, bleu cheese or curry dressing. **$3.95**
☺ Topped with cheese, mushrooms and green peppers. **$5.95**

CAESAR PLEASER
Perhaps if Caesar had held the anchovies like we do, he might have made it through the Ides of March. A tradition. **$3.95**
☺ With a grilled, marinated chicken breast **$5.95**

THAI CHICKEN SALAD
Lettuce and oriental vegetables topped with our grilled chicken breast marinated in soy, ginger and tasty spices. **$6.95**

LUNCHBOX SALADS
Salads you used to trade for at school, made better. Choose white albacore tuna, tangy chicken or bay shrimp salad, served on a bed of seasonal greens with tomatoes and hard-boiled eggs. **$4.95**
☺ With fresh avocado **$5.95**

ZOOT SUIT FRUIT
Sure, this is a traditional seasonal fruit plate, served with a raspberry yogurt dipping sauce. But we got your attention, didn't we? **$5.95**

MARY'S SOUP DU JOUR
Imagine Mary slaving over a caldron of hot, stick-to-your-ribs homemade soup. Served with a honey wheat roll. Think how she'd feel if you didn't have some.
Cup **$2.25** Bowl **$3.95**

MARY'S COMMUNE CHILI
Ah, the '60s. Life was spicier, if you know what we mean. This chili sums it up: Simmered slowly, groovily spiced and very, very nice, man. Topped with cheese and chopped onions.
Cup **$2.50** Bowl **$3.25**

Soups & Salads

restaurant
The Family Buggy Restaurant

location
Farmington, Michigan

designer
Donald Payne

year produced
1988

CONCEPT

Because The Family Buggy Restaurant draws a large lunch crowd that consists mostly of families with children, a new room was designed for adults only. Complete with oak and brass cages, this room has an antique bank interior theme.

The menus were designed around this bank theme. The owner designed the menus from bank book covers, as he found his was so durable. The covers have proven almost indestructible. A dessert menu, printed to look like money, sticks out of the bank book.

SPECIAL VISUAL EFFECTS

Few things attract as much attention as money sticking out of a bank book laying on a table. It is a great tie-in with a room that literally has a 1800s bank at one end. Guests go to the tellers' window to pay their check, which has "DEPOSIT TICKET" printed on its back in big letters.

paper stock
80# Cover, Simpson Starwhite Vicksburg, Natural White

typefaces
Galliard Roman, Bold, Italic

number of color inks
One

number produced
50 *(per printing)*

DIVIDENDS

PEPPERMINT FUDGE HIGH PIE
Creamy peppermint ice cream and rich hot fudge set in a graham cracker crust.
$2.45

GENUINE
"KATHY'S" CHEESECAKE
Topped with strawberries.
$2.45

DUTCH APPLE PIE
$1.75
With ice cream, add .40

GOLF BALL
HOT FUDGE SUNDAE
If you're too full for dessert but 'need' some chocolate...Guaranteed small.
$.95

MO'S CARAMEL TREAT
French puff pastry filled with butter pecan ice cream and topped with whipped topping and caramel sauce.
$2.45

GREAT SUNDAES
Chocolate, strawberry, hot fudge or caramel.
Reg. $1.95 Lg. $2.45

ICE CREAM & SHERBETS
1.65

12/92

FAMILY BUGGY RESTAURANTS, INC.

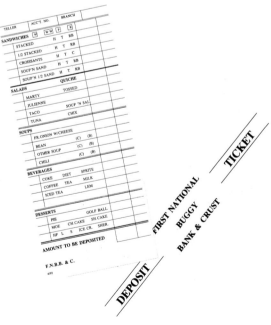

restaurant
Horsefeathers

location
North Conway, New Hampshire

design firm
Glen Group Marketing & Advertising

designer
Maureen Rupprecht

illustrators
Jodi Neal *(hand illustration)*
Gayle Lemerise *(computer generated illustration)*
Maureen Rupprecht *(computer generated illustration)*

copywriter
Donna Stuart

year produced
1993

CONCEPT

Horsefeathers' menu is informational, comprehensive and durable. Aside from being a good representative of the restaurant's ambiance, it is also easily coordinated with the restaurant's decor.

The menu has an advertising format, which in addition to giving the restaurant a "neighborhood" feel, allows the restaurant to change their menus periodically, as the advertisements cover the cost of production and printing. The left hand side of the menus are formatted with full-color ads, while the right hand pages are subdued, bringing more attention to the ads. The menu is also laminated, which provides durability.

paper stock
12pt Coated with Two-side Laminate

typefaces
Friz Quadrata *(menu pages)*
Goudy Extra Bold, Times *(ad pages)*

number of color inks
Four

number produced
400

design budget
$1,700

Kids of All Ages

restaurant
The Italian Oven

location
Latrobe, Pennsylvania

design firm
The Italian Oven, Inc.

designer
Janet M. Buccianelli

illustrator
A.J. Frye

copywriter
The Italian Oven, Inc.

year produced
1992

CONCEPT

With graphics drawn by a child, this menu for The Italian Oven invites children to choose their meal in a manner that is appealing to them. The design is very colorful and fun to look at from a child's point of view.

SPECIAL VISUAL EFFECTS

Throughout the menu, animals serve the kids' food, and play inside the restaurant. The menu also includes renderings of the Italian Oven's "ovens" and checkerboard borders.

TRENDS FOR THE '90s

"Menus will be simpler in concept, more direct and appealing to customers on a variety of levels."

paper stock
80# White Fortune Gloss Cover

typeface
Handwritten

printing technique
Offset Lithography

number of color inks
Four-color Process with Two Metallics

number produced
10,000

design budget
$20,000–$30,000

restaurant
Disney's Polynesian Resort Restaurant

location
**Walt Disney World,
Lake Buena Vista, Florida**

design firm
Walt Disney World Resort Design

designer
Mimi Palladino

illustrator
Peter Emslie

year produced
1992

CONCEPT

The designers have created a kids' menu that features a Walt Disney film and provides an activity to occupy children while they wait for their meal. Disney's Polynesian Resort Restaurant features lush floral landscapes, and so the *Jungle Book* was chosen because of its tropical setting.

SPECIAL EFFECTS

When folded, the characters Mowgli, Baloo and Kaa are shown at the end of a dinner table. Unfolded, all the main characters appear, sharing a long stone table set in the jungle. The characters interact with each other, making eating fun.

Turn the menu over and the child can pop out Kaa, the snake, color him, and coil him to wear as a snake hat. This provides a fun activity for kids as well as a souvenir to wear after they leave the restaurant.

TRENDS FOR THE '90s

"Although not used for this particular menu, we see laser printing of menu copy will be on the increase because of the flexibility it gives the restaurant operator for change."

paper stock
Simpson Starwhite Vicksburg

typeface
Lithos

printing technique
Offset Lithography, Die-cut

number of color inks
Four

number produced
30,000

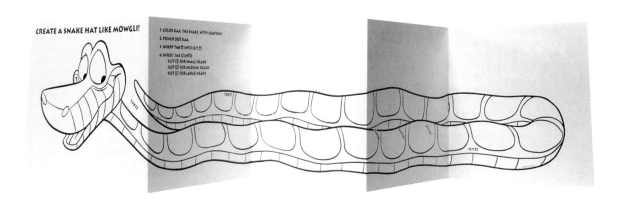

restaurant
Stars

location
Hingham, Massachusetts

design firm
Marie P. Flaherty Arts & Design

designer/illustrator
Marie Flaherty Henderson

copywriter
Edward Kane

paper stock
Simpson Gainsborough Frost White

typefaces
Triset *(heads)*
Frutiger Condensed *(body copy)*

printing technique
Offset Two-color Kamori Sprint

number of color inks
Three PMS

number produced
100

CONCEPT

Stars' children's menu incorporates the design elements of the regular menu in terms of colors and the human and animal figures used. The children's menu is in place mat form.

TRENDS FOR THE '90s

"I see a disturbing trend in today's menu design. I see no DESIGN. With personal computers and the advent of cheap color copying, many restaurants are by-passing designers, and therefore, good design...."

Children's Menu

★ ★ ★

Breakfast

two pancakes	1.95	
w/meat	2.50	
cereal	1.25	
fruit loops, cheerios		
child's french toast	1.95	
w/meat	2.50	

Lunch/Dinner

pasta	3.95
w/homemade tomato sauce	
homemade chicken fingers	3.95
chicken wings	3.95
grilled cheese	2.50
w/tomato	2.75
w/bacon & tomato	3.00
tuna fish sandwich	2.95
chicken salad sandwich	3.25
fish & chips	4.95
1/4 lb burger	3.95
w/cheese	4.25
grilled chicken	4.75
teriyaki or bbq	
6" boboli pizza	
cheese	3.50
pepperoni	3.95
sausage	3.95
pepper & onion	3.95
canadian bacon	3.95
vegetable	3.95

all of the above Lunch and Dinner entrees are prepared with lots of love. all items come served with fries except for the pizza and the pasta.

Desserts

jr. hot fudge sundae	1.95
ice cream	1.50
jr. strawberry shortcake	1.95

this menu is for children only. proper i.d. not required.

we hope you enjoy **STARS**.

150

restaurant
Narcoosee's Restaurant
(Grand Floridian Resort)

location
**Walt Disney World,
Lake Buena Vista, Florida**

design firm
Walt Disney World Design

designer
Mimi Palladino

illustrator
Peter Emslie

copywriter
Tony Fernandez

year produced
1993

CONCEPT

Narcoosee's Restaurant overlooks Seven Seas Lagoon. Its menu primarily features seafood, including an alligator appetizer. The kids' menu provides children with a unique and exciting activity, as well as a souvenir to take home.

SPECIAL VISUAL EFFECTS

Unfolded, the menu features a full-color image of the alligator Brutus (from *The Rescuers*), seen from above on the front of the menu and from beneath on the back. Brutus pops out and folds into a three-dimensional alligator. The menu copy is printed on the gator's belly so that if kids pop out their gator before ordering their meal, they can still read the menu.

paper stock
Quintessence Remarque

typeface
Lithos

printing technique
Offset Lithography, Die-cut

number of color inks
Four

number produced
20,000

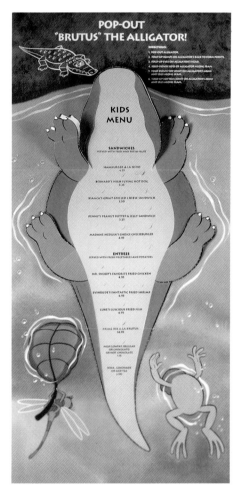

restaurant
Cucina! Cucina!

location
Seattle, Washington

design firm
Aardvark Graphics

designer/illustrator
Kevin Atteberny

year produced
1990

CONCEPT

Cucina Charlie is a friendly fire-breathing dragon, and Cucina! Cucina!'s mascot. He was chosen because the restaurant's signature is a wood-burning oven. The menu features Cucina Charlie in an activity and coloring book designed to keep children busy.

SPECIAL VISUAL EFFECTS

The front page of the coloring book was colored-in with crayons.

©Schwartz Brothers Restaurants, 1990

152

restaurant
Holiday Inns *(28 Canada Locations)*

location
Etobicoke, Ontario, Canada

design firm
Morris Graphics Ltd.

art director/copywriter
Michael Moran

designer/illustrator
Jim Craig

year produced
1991

CONCEPT

An alternative to the traditional comic book style menu, Holiday Inns' Johnny Holiday menu is fun, interesting and educational, filled with anecdotes to keep kids occupied. Designed as an activity wheel game, Mr. Hippo asks questions about endangered species, and Wise Owl provides the answers.

SPECIAL EFFECTS

The activity wheel spins.

TRENDS FOR THE '90s

"Kids' menus/activities will grow in popularity and importance. They will be timely, topical and educational in subject and have strong graphic impact and appeal. They (will) offer strong opportunities for cross promotions and sponsorship between suppliers and restaurant."

paper stock
12pt Cornwall C2S

typefaces
Hand Lettering, Helvetica

printing technique
Offset Lithography

number of color inks
Four

number produced
50,000

PHOTOGRAPHY COURTESY OF COMMONWEALTH HOSPITALITY LTD.

153

restaurant
Friendly's

design firm
The Menu Workshop

designers
Liz Kearney
Margo Christianson
Steve Grundmeyer

illustrator/photographer
Steven Hone

copywriters
Friendly's
The Menu Workshop

year produced
1993

CONCEPT

Friendly's children's menu is part of an overall program designed to upgrade the restaurant within their current niche: family dining. The menu educates children about food while they have fun. A two-sided place mat format, the back is filled with games and educational facts, and the front contains menu items enhanced with playful characters.

TRENDS FOR THE '90s

"Computers make production easier (cheaper), so more colors are available. Short run colors can be done on laser printers. Recycled papers are a must for environmentally friendly restaurants. Whole programs—menu, logo, ads, interior—are now easier to coordinate with computers."

paper stock
Coated House Stock

printing technique
Offset Lithography

number of color inks
Six

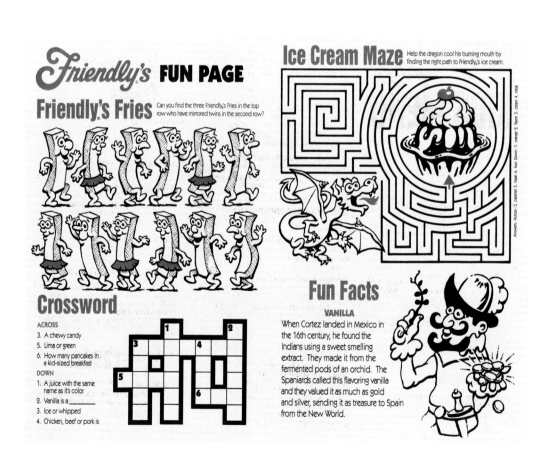

CONCEPT

This menu is intended to inform and to entertain. It has an educational aspect because it encourages close reading, and upon reading it delivers a subtle humorous message.

SPECIAL VISUAL EFFECTS

Simple lettering, whimsical doodles, fun colors.

TRENDS FOR THE '90s

" 'Children' are out and 'kids' are in, and nineties kids are sophisticated customers. Grinning tortoises and trains tend to offend a portion of the market that these menus intend to reach. As modern food knowledge evolves, concise descriptions will be in demand. The future is information and creativity."

restaurant
El Torito Restaurants, Inc.

location
Irvine, California

designer/illustrator
Deborah Collins

copywriter
Wes Clark

year produced
1992

CONCEPT

Appealing to all age groups, El Torito's children's menu features fun games with educational value. The menu's comic book style format contains the story of a family of peppers that children can color in with their "peppers" crayons. The story in the comic book relates facts about Mexico.

TRENDS FOR THE '90s

"The computer will continue to allow greater freedom both timewise and financially with regard to menu production, especially for the smaller non-chain restaurants. In contrast, I think the handmade, beautifully crafted type of menu will continue to be popular."

paper stock
Web 50# Crownbrite White Text

typefaces
Brody Script, Futura Condensed

printing technique
Offset Lithography

number of color inks
Four-color Process

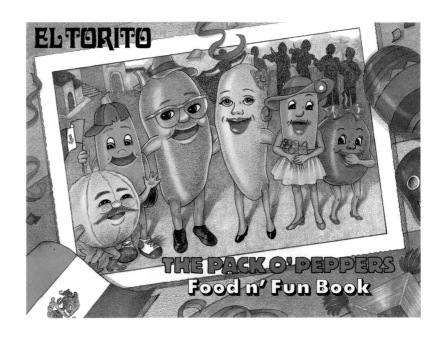

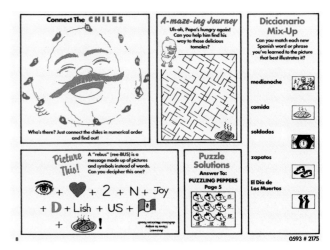

restaurant
Hotel Principe Felipe

location
Le Manga, Spain

design firm
David Carter Design

art director/designer
Lori Wilson

illustrators
various children

copywriter
Hotel Principe Felipe

year produced
1993

CONCEPT
At 5" x 5", Hotel Principe Felipe's children's menu is the perfect size for small hands. The menu folds out, and playful illustrations drawn by various children present the items on the menu.

paper stock
Simpson Starwhite Vicksburg

typefaces
Futura, Caslon

printing technique
Offset Lithography

number of color inks
Four-color Process, Two PMS

number produced
250

restaurant
Newport Bay Club

location
Euro Disney, Paris, France

design firm
David Carter Design

designer
Lori Wilson

illustrator
Larry Sons

year produced
1992

CONCEPT

Euro Disney's Newport Bay Club's children's menus are set up for mix-and-match card games. Menu items appear on one side of this perforated card menu, and nautical illustrations appear on the other.

paper stock
Simpson Starwhite Vicksburg

typeface
Willow

printing technique
Offset Lithography

number of color inks
Four PMS

number produced
500

158

restaurant
Black-Eyed Pea

location
Dallas, Texas

design firm
The Baker Agency

designer/illustrator
Jim Foster

copywriter
Mikie Baker

year produced
1993

CONCEPT

Family-oriented Black-Eyed Pea wanted to give children a bright and colorful form of entertainment while dining. Throughout the menu, a set of identifiable characters, The Peabody's, have adventures that change to hold children's attention. Cups and specialty items are designed to induce children back into the restaurants.

The games on both the front and back of the place mat are designed for five- to seven-year-olds and the back of the place mat is overly busy to hold attention for a longer period of time. The menu is included on the place mat for ease of ordering.

TRENDS FOR THE '90s

"Marketing to children is becoming extremely aggressive and competitive. You can no longer hand out a place mat filled with simple games. Today the restaurateur must develop characters, logos, clubs, and special offers to compete."

paper stock
Finish Stock/Web

typefaces
Tekton, Helvetica, Windsor

printing technique
Web Printing

number of color inks
Four

number produced
3,000

design budget
$6,500

restaurant
Tony's Town Square Restaurant

location
**Walt Disney World,
Lake Buena Vista, Florida**

design firm
Walt Disney World Design

designer
Mimi Palladino

illustrators
Peter Emslie *(Breakfast, Lunch/Dinner)*
Russ Russell *(Lunch/Dinner)*

year produced
1993

CONCEPT

Tony's Town Square Restaurant's children's breakfast menu is designed to look like an authentic newspaper's comics section and features a story about the characters Lady and the Tramp. The menu items, games and activities are on the back.

The children's lunch and dinner menu pops-out into a three-dimensional replica of the restaurant. The *Lady and the Tramp* characters pop out and can stand like paper dolls.

BREAKFAST

paper stock
French Durotone

typefaces
Goudy, Times Roman

printing technique
Straight One-Color Shot

LUNCH/DINNER

paper stock
Warren Lustro Gloss

typefaces
Snell, Roundhand, Goudy

printing technique
Four-color Process, Die-cuts

number of color inks
Four

number produced
30,000

WALT DISNEY WORLD DESIGN

restaurant
Grand Floridian Cafe
(Disney's Grand Floridian Resort)

location
**Walt Disney World,
Lake Buena Vista, Florida**

design firm
Walt Disney World Design

designer
Dale Moore

illustrator
Al Carroll

copywriter
Greg Ehrbar

year produced
1988

CONCEPT

Disney's Grand Floridian Resort and its restaurant's menus are designed to replicate the Victorian Era, giving guests the experience of going back in time. Reinforcing this concept, this children's menu provides a toy representative of that era. Pointers on how to build sandcastles are given inside the menu, and a pocket on the opposite page holds a list of menu items and two paper dolls, each outfitted with an array of clothing. One even has her own baby carriage and doll.

TRENDS FOR THE '90s

"Changeable menus using laser printed inserts. This allows (the) restaurant operator to be very spontaneous with the food offered as he can change the menu instantly."

paper stock
Beckett RSVP, Cameo Dull

typefaces
Hand Lettering *(headlines)*
Artcraft Regular *(body copy)*

printing technique
Offset Lithography, Die-cut

number of color inks
Four-color Process

number produced
30,000 *(per year)*

AT THE BEACH

PAPER DOLLS
Grand Floridian Beach Resort

HOW TO BUILD SANDCASTLES

You can build your own dream castle at the beach. Find a moist sand area to build on, not too close to the water. Pack mounds of sand together by hand or in a pail. Nice, firm mounds of sand can be carved with sticks, spoons or your fingers. Sprinkling a little water on the sand will keep it from crumbling. Perhaps you have really seen a magical castle some where. Now you can build it out of sand.

MENU

Appetizers

Fresh Fruit Cup $1.50

Entrées

Boneless Fried Chicken Strips with Fries $3.95

Fried Fish Nuggets with Fries $4.25

Pasta with Meat Sauce $3.25

Kid Burger with Fries $3.95
With Cheese $4.25

Peanut Butter and Jelly Sandwich
on Whole Wheat with Chips $2.50

Kid-Size Frank on a Bun with Chips $2.50

Desserts

Ice Cream or Sherbet $1.75
Strawberry or Chocolate Sundae $2.75
Children 11 and under

Grand Floridian Beach Resort

restaurant
Boston Pizza

location
Vancouver, Canada

design firm
Blue Suede Studio

designer
Dave Kennedy

illustrators
Scott Schneider
Derik Murray

copywriters
Enn Jurgenson
Greg Lamone

year produced
1993

CONCEPT

The design of the menu focuses on the three things that are the pillars of success of Boston Pizza: pasta, pizza, and their customers. The children's menu features playful characters and graphics.

TRENDS FOR THE '90s

"Menus will be more flexible to allow for product updates and will be more customer-friendly."

restaurant
Elephant Bar

location
Santa Barbara, California

design firm
Visual Events

art director
Mari Jo Pelzner

designer
Richard Couch

illustrator
Gary Johnson

year produced
1992

CONCEPT

A humorous menu was designed to entertain children while families enjoy a meal together at the Elephant Bar.

paper stock
70# White Mustang Offset Wove

typefaces
Modula Serif Bold, Times, Garamond

printing technique
Offset Lithography

number of color inks
Four

number produced
72,000

Kids Menu & Adventure Book

For kids 10 years and younger. Includes a glass of milk or soda and a small ice cream sundae.

Elephant Kid's Burger $2.95
With lettuce, tomato and French fries.

Chicken Tenders $2.95
Lightly breaded and golden fried with French fries and honey mustard sauce.

Grilled Cheese Sandwich $2.95
Melted cheddar cheese on grilled whole wheat, served with French fries.

Corn Dog $2.95
With French fries.

Spaghetti with Meat Sauce $2.95

Chicken Quesadilla $2.95

163

Bottoms Up!

restaurant
Eureka!

location
Dallas, Texas

design firm
Powell Design

designers
Glyn Powell
Dorit Suffness
Jon Buell

illustrators
Glyn Powell
Dorit Suffness

year produced
1993

CONCEPT

The name "Eureka!" comes from the idea that this restaurant would be a place to discover new and interesting foods and coffees. The design incorporates a black-and-white checked motif because the client loves black-and-white checks.

TRENDS FOR THE '90s

"Recycled papers and soy inks. Anything else is unappetizing."

paper stock
Various

typeface
Futura Bold & Condensed Ultra Bold

printing technique
Offset Lithography, Silkscreen

number of color inks
One

Something's Brewing!
a l l   a b o u t   c o f f e e

GRAND OPENING!

Now that we're open,

come join the fun with a taste of Eureka!

Joanne Levy and Lisa Kramer

will welcome you Sunday, August 8,

from 7 to 9 p.m.

You'll discover a deliciously grand time.

4011 Villanova
(East of Preston Road in The Plaza At Preston Center)
Dallas, Texas 75225 214.369.7797

Eureka! went to the Great Pacific Northwest – the nation's leading coffee region – to find the perfect coffees. We chose Coffee Bean International of Portland, Oregon as our roaster because they too share our commitment to quality. They offer us the superlative of the world's finest Arabica coffees.

Eureka!'s staff is extensively trained to ensure that our customers receive knowledgeable service that matches the quality of our coffee.

Every piece of coffee brewing equipment we sell at Eureka! has been tested and evaluated. We continue to test and monitor new devices as they come on the market.

Brewing the Perfect Cup

1) Use freshly drawn cold tap water in a scrupulously clean pot. Consider using a water filter or bottled water, as your cup of coffee is only as good as the water that's used to make it. If using a manual device, use water that is just "off" the boil so as not to "burn" the coffee.

2) We recommend using 1 Teaspoon of ground coffee per cup for a light cup up to 2 Teaspoons for a heavier, stronger cup.

3) Use the proper grind for your coffee equipment. Our Eureka! staff will gladly guide you. Often, If your coffee is bitter and overly strong, the grind is too fine or you have used too much coffee. If the brew lacks flavor or strength, it is likely that the grind is too coarse or you have used too little coffee. We will happily provide you a sample to take home as a grinding guide of the appropriate grind for your machine.

4) For best results, brew to the full capacity of your coffee maker.

5) For best flavor, don't reheat cooled coffee or allow it to sit on a heat source for over 20 minutes.

6) To prevent bitterness, never re-use grounds.

7) An air pot, such as a thermos or any other kind of vacuum container with a glass or stainless steel interior, will keep freshly brewed coffee warm for a long time.

8) We recommend storing coffee in an airtight container in the refrigerator or freezer. For best results, grind the amount of coffee needed just prior to brewing. Remember air is coffee's #1 enemy!

These four basic characteristics work together in harmony to produce the total coffee experience.

Body: Refers to weight, consistency or viscosity of the brew. Its the impression of the weight of the brew on your tongue.

Acidity: The tartness or liveliness of the coffee. It sharpens and brings special flavors into focus.

Flavor: The intensity of the inherent flavor qualities of coffee which may be dependent on the bean, soil in which it was grown, and milling and roasting processes.

Aroma: The delicate nuances that emit from brewed coffee and the effect that has on the overall taste.

restaurant
Red Robin Restaurants

location
Irvine, California

design firm
Claude Prettyman Design

designer
Claude Prettyman

photographer
Tom Pasini

copywriter
Wes Clark

year produced
1993

CONCEPT

Red Robin's menu incorporates the restaurant's primary color palette and variety of food and drink. The inside spread lists all the options so the diner doesn't have to turn the page. Therefore the menu is fun, colorful, and easy to read.

Simple bold color and graphics create an easily identifiable carry-out package.

The seasonal menu features drinks and entrees with a Jamaican theme. Bright colors and rough-edged graphics complement the products. The character presents a playful way to tie in the summer with the food and drinks.

paper stock
Productolith

typefaces
VAG Rounded, Lithos

printing technique
Offset Lithography, Laminated

number of color inks
Six

restaurant
Top of Toronto *(CN Tower)*

location
Toronto, Ontario, Canada

design firm
Morris Graphics Ltd.

designer/illustrator
Harvey Sedlack

year produced
1992

CONCEPT

The CN Tower is the world's tallest free-standing structure and one of Canada's premier tourist attractions. Therefore, the wine list for its Top of Toronto restaurant had many objectives to fill.

The multi-language composition of the restaurant suggested the use of wine labels in the menu for easy recognition and comfort for users. Effective graphic symbols help identify the country of origin and brief descriptions make selecting wines easier, no matter where you may be from. Recognizable wines from around the world further enhance the comfort level. The wine list is presented in two different languages—French and English.

TRENDS FOR THE '90s

"People's fascination with wines and food will continue. Use your menu to educate them, stimulate them and satisfy them with good quality and variety of products."

paper stock
8pt Strathmore Grande Cover Cornwall

typeface
Palatino Italic

printing technique
Offset Lithography

number of color inks
Four-color Process

number produced
1,000

170

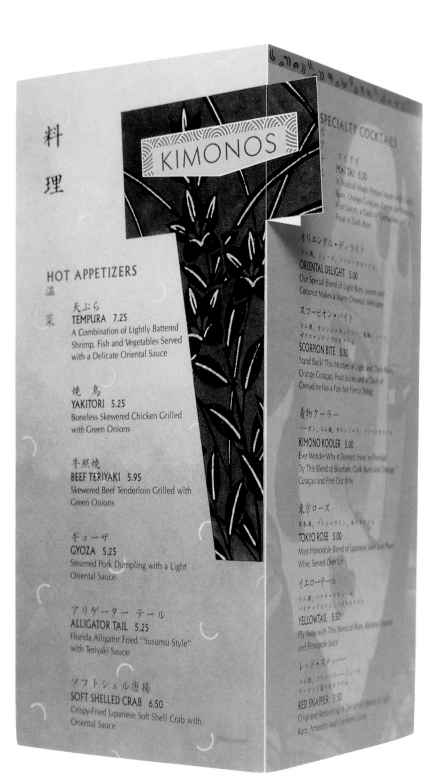

restaurant
Kimono's *(Westin Swan Hotel)*

location
Orlando, Florida

design firm
Associates Design

art director
Charles Polonsky

designers
Beth Finn
Jill Arena
Donna Sommerville

illustrator
Beth Finn

year produced
1992

CONCEPT

The Kimono's tent card successfully embodies Japanese ambiance with its simplicity and elegance. Die-cut Japanese elements on one panel flow into the following panel creating interest, beauty and continuity. Each panel on the four-sided three-dimensional piece presents a design with copy that can stand alone.

paper stock
12pt Carolina Cover C1S

typeface
Albertus

printing technique
Offset Lithography

number of color inks
Four-color Process
Two-color Imprint

number produced
1,000

restaurant
Hyatt Hotels and Resorts

location
Chicago, Illinois

design firm
Associates Design

art director
Charles Polonsky

designer/illustrator
Beth Finn

year produced
1993

CONCEPT

A cubist style and bright colors communicate elements of summer and support the menu's theme, "Iced Cubism."

SPECIAL VISUAL EFFECTS

The illustration was printed on U.V. paper and filters a ghosted mirror image on the other side. Drink selections, printed on the ghosted interior, are tailored to fit the theme of the promotion.

paper stock
U.V. Ultra

typefaces
Univers, Fenice, Burlington

printing technique
Offset Lithography

number of color ink
Four-color Process

number produced
20,000

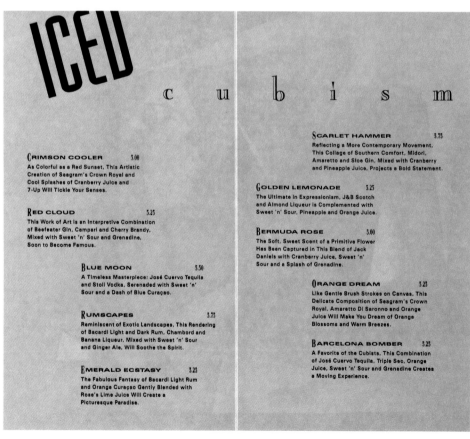

ICED cubism

CRIMSON COOLER 3.00
As Colorful as a Red Sunset, This Artistic Creation of Seagram's Crown Royal and Cool Splashes of Cranberry Juice and 7-Up Will Tickle Your Senses.

RED CLOUD 3.25
This Work of Art is an Interpretive Combination of Beefeater Gin, Campari and Cherry Brandy, Mixed with Sweet 'n' Sour and Grenadine, Soon to Become Famous.

BLUE MOON 3.50
A Timeless Masterpiece: José Cuervo Tequila and Stoli Vodka, Serenaded with Sweet 'n' Sour and a Dash of Blue Curaçao.

RUMSCAPES 3.75
Reminiscent of Exotic Landscapes, This Rendering of Bacardi Light and Dark Rum, Chambord and Banana Liqueur, Mixed with Sweet 'n' Sour and Ginger Ale, Will Soothe the Spirit.

EMERALD ECSTASY 3.25
The Fabulous Fantasy of Bacardi Light Rum and Orange Curaçao Gently Blended with Rose's Lime Juice Will Create a Picturesque Paradise.

SCARLET HAMMER 3.75
Reflecting a More Contemporary Movement, This Collage of Southern Comfort, Midori, Amaretto and Sloe Gin, Mixed with Cranberry and Pineapple Juice, Projects a Bold Statement.

GOLDEN LEMONADE 3.25
The Ultimate in Expressionism, J&B Scotch and Almond Liqueur is Complemented with Sweet 'n' Sour, Pineapple and Orange Juice.

BERMUDA ROSE 3.00
The Soft, Sweet Scent of a Primitive Flower Has Been Captured in This Blend of Jack Daniels with Cranberry Juice, Sweet 'n' Sour and a Splash of Grenadine.

ORANGE DREAM 3.25
Like Gentle Brush Strokes on Canvas, This Delicate Composition of Seagram's Crown Royal, Amaretto Di Saronno and Orange Juice Will Make You Dream of Orange Blossoms and Warm Breezes.

BARCELONA BOMBER 3.25
A Favorite of the Cubists, This Combination of José Cuervo Tequila, Triple Sec, Orange Juice, Sweet 'n' Sour and Grenadine Creates a Moving Experience.

172

restaurant
57th Street Bar *(Hotel New York)*

location
Euro Disney, Paris, France

design firm
David Carter Design

designer/illustrator
Sharon LeJeune

year produced
1992

CONCEPT

The 57th Street Bar's menu is designed to reflect the elegant 1930s ambiance of the Hotel New York.

TRENDS FOR THE '90s

"Flexibility. It's what most restaurants and chefs want today. The ability to easily change out items and add fresh new dishes on a regular basis...."

typeface
Futura

printing technique
Offset Lithography

number of color inks
Three PMS

number produced
2,000

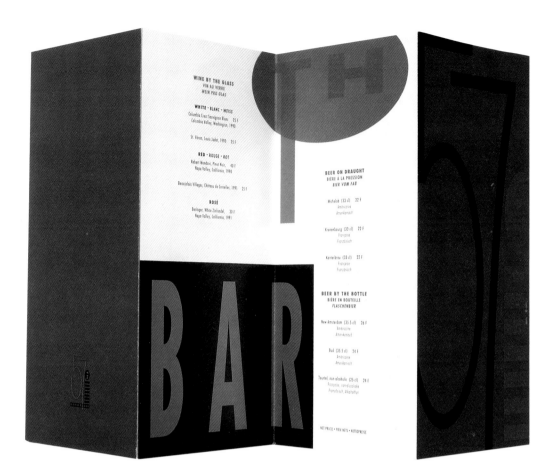

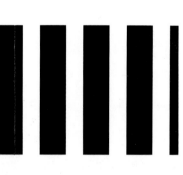

SPECIALTY COCKTAILS
COCKTAILS MAISON
COCKTAILS NACH ART DES HAUSES

AMERICAN KIR   40 F
Whidbey's Loganberry Liqueur with Domaine Ste. Michelle Sparkling Wine
Whidbey's Liqueur de "Loganberry" et du vin pétillant Domaine Ste. Michelle
Likör aus Loganbeeren mit Sekt, Domaine Ste. Michelle

DECO DELIGHT   50 F
Peach Schnapps and Orange Juice on the Rocks
Schnapps à la pêche, jus d'orange glacé
Pfirsichschnapps, Orangensaft und Eis

BIG APPLE   70 F
Apple Jack Brandy with Triple Sec and Champagne
Brandy Apple Jack, triple sec et champagne
Cognac Apple Jack, Triple Sec and Champagner

UPTOWN EXPRESS   50 F
Vodka and Crème de Cacao with Cream
Vodka, crème de cacao et crème
Wodka, Kakaocreme und Sahne

WALL STREET HUSTLER   50 F
Scotch with Sweet and Dry Vermouth
Scotch au vermouth sec et doux
Scotch mit trockenem und süßem Wermut

SPECIALTY COCKTAILS WITHOUT THE ALCOHOL
COCKTAILS MAISON NON ALCOOLISÉS
COCKTAILS NACH ART DES HAUSES OHNE ALKOHOL

OLD FASHIONED LEMONADE   20 F
Limonade à l'ancienne
Traditionelle Zitronenlimonade

LIGHTS OF BROADWAY   22 F
Sparkling Water and Cranberry Juice
Eau gazeuse et jus d'airelle
Mineralwasser und Preiselbeerensaft

VIRGIN MARY   24 F
Jus de tomate et jus de citron assaisonnés
Tomatensaft mit gewürztem Zitronensaft

SHIRLEY TEMPLE   15 F
Ginger ale avec un doigt de grenadine "on the rocks"
Ginger Ale mit einem Spritzer Grenadine und Eis

SCREWDRIVER   40 F
Mélange classique de vodka et de jus d'orange
Die klassische Kombination aus Wodka und Orangensaft

LONG ISLAND ICE TEA   50 F
A smooth blend of Rum, Gin, Vodka, Tequila and Triple Sec
with a Splash of Coca-Cola and Citrus Flavor
Un doux mélange de rhum, gin, vodka, tequila et triple sec
avec un jet de coca-cola et un parfum de citron
*Eine milde Mischung aus Rum, Gin, Wodka, Tequila und Triple Sec
mit einem Spritzer Coca-Cola und Zitronenaroma*

BLOODY MARY   40 F
Jus de tomate, citron, tabasco et vodka
Tomatensaft, Zitrone, Tabasco und Wodka

CENTRAL SPARK   50 F
Fresh Squeezed Orange Juice, Sparkling Wine and a Blush of Cassis
Orange pressée, vin pétillant et un doigt de cassis
Frisch gepreßter Orangensaft, Sekt und ein Spritzer schwarze Johannisbeere

AMERICAN SPARKLING WINE
VIN PÉTILLANT AMÉRICAIN
AMERIKANISCHER SEKT

DOMAINE CARNEROS, TAITTINGER, NAPA VALLEY N.V.
by the Glass • au verre • *pro Glas (18 cl)*   45 F
by the Bottle • en bouteille • *pro Flasche (750 ml)*   200 F

DOMAINE CHANDON BRUT, NAPA VALLEY N.V.
by the Bottle • en bouteille • *pro Flasche (750 ml)*   160 F

MAISON DEUTZ BRUT CUVÉE, NAPA VALLEY N.V.
by the Glass • au verre • *pro Glas (18 cl)*   35 F
by the Bottle • en bouteille • *pro Flasche (750 ml)*   170 F

CHAMPAGNE

TAITTINGER BRUT "LA FRANÇAISE" N.V.
by the Glass • au verre • *pro Glas (12 cl)*   60 F
by the Bottle • en bouteille • *pro Flasche (750 ml)*   275 F

MOËT & CHANDON BRUT N.V.
by the Glass • au verre • *pro Glas (12 cl)*   55 F
by the Bottle • en bouteille • *pro Flasche (750 ml)*   260 F

DEUTZ BLANC DE BLANCS 1985
by the bottle • en bouteille • *pro Flasche (750 ml)*   450 F

restaurant
Spike's Jazz Bar *(Hotel Principe Felipe)*

location
Murcia, Spain

design firm
David Carter Design

art director
Lori Wilson

designers
Lori Wilson
Gary LoBue, Jr.

illustrator
Gary LoBue, Jr.

copywriter
Hotel Principe Felipe

year produced
1993

CONCEPT
The beverage menus for Spike's Jazz Bar
are exciting, colorful and freeform like jazz,
with a flexible format that allows beverage
selections to change easily.

paper stock
Simpson Starwhite Vicksburg

typeface
Futura

printing technique
Offset Lithography

number of color inks
Six PMS

number produced
500

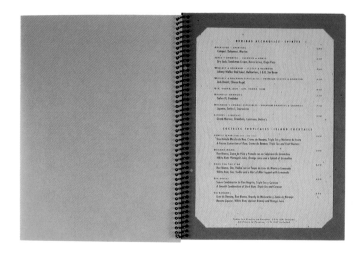

restaurant
Redwood Bar and Lounge *(Sequoia Lounge)*

location
Euro Disney, Paris, France

design firm
David Carter Design

designer/illustrator
David Brashier

photographer
David Meunch

year produced
1992

CONCEPT

Redwood Bar and Lounge's menu was designed for the pool area of the Sequoia Lounge at Euro Disney. Both the lounge and the hotel were named for the forests of Northern California, and this theme is reflected in the design of the lounge's logo and menu. Enormous redwood trees are depicted on the beverage menu, and on the tables in triangular wood bases.

paper stock
Curtis Tuscan Terra

typefaces
Trajan, Bodoni

printing technique
Offset Lithography

number of color inks
Three *(on each side)*

number produced
1,000

SPECIALTY COCKTAILS WITHOUT ALCOHOL
COCKTAILS SANS ALCOOL · COCKTAILS OHNE ALKOHOL

OLD FASHIONED LEMONADE 20F
Limonade à l'ancienne
Traditionelle Zitronenlimonade

BEAR HUG 32F
FRESH STRAWBERRIES AND FRESH ORANGE JUICE WITH HONEY
Fraises et jus d'orange pressée avec du miel
Frischer Orangensaft und Erdbeeren mit Honig

REDWOOD 28F
CRANBERRY JUICE AND FRESH ORANGE JUICE OVER ICE
Jus d'orange et d'airelle on the rocks
Preiselbeer- und frischer Orangensaft auf Eis

HIKER'S REWARD 25F
PINEAPPLE JUICE AND ROSE'S LIME JUICE, ON THE ROCKS
Jus d'ananas et de citron vert on the rocks
Ananas- und Limonensaft auf Eis

SPECIALTY COCKTAILS
COCKTAILS MAISON
COCKTAILS NACH ART DES HAUSES

AMERICAN KIR 40F
Whidbey's liqueur de "loganberry" et
vin pétillant, Domaine Ste. Michelle
Likör aus Loganbeeren mit
Sekt Domaine Ste. Michelle

OL' GRIZZLY 50F
VODKA AND KAHLUA OVER ICE
Vodka et Kahlua on the rocks
Wodka und Kahlua auf Eis

YOSEMITE SUNRISE 40F
TEQUILA WITH FRESH ORANGE JUICE AND GRENADINE
Tequila, orange pressée et grenadine
Tequila mit frischem Orangen- und Grenadinensaft

MAKING TRACKS 50F
LIME JUICE, TRIPLE SEC AND VODKA
Jus de citron vert, triple sec et vodka
Limonensaft, Triple Sec und Wodka

BLIZZARD 40F
RUM AND PINEAPPLE JUICE, SERVED ICE COLD
Rhum et jus d'ananas glacé
Rum und Ananassaft, eisgekühlt serviert

TIMBERLAND 40F
SOUR AT ITS BEST: BLENDED WHISKEY AND LEMON JUICE
Acide à souhait: mélange de whisky et jus de citron
"Sauer" von seiner besten Seite: Whiskyverschnitt und Zitronensaft

WINES BY THE GLASS
VINS AU VERRE · WEINE PRO GLAS

WHITE WINE · VIN BLANC · WEIßWEIN
Beringer Chardonnay, Napa, 1989 25F
Château de Moncontour, Vouvray, 1989 25F

RED WINE · VIN ROUGE · ROTWEIN
Sequoia Grove Cabernet Sauvignon, Napa, 1987 25F
Château Bellegrave Cru Bourgeois, Pauillac, 1986 25F

BEERS · BIÈRES · BIERE

DRAUGHT · À LA PRESSION · VOM FASS
Michelob (33 cl) 22F   Kanterbräu (33 cl) 22F
Kronenbourg (33 cl) 22F

BOTTLED · EN BOUTEILLE · FLASCHENBIER
Bud (33.5 cl) 24F   Samuel Adams (35.5 cl) 26F
Coors (35.5 cl) 24F   Kronenbourg 1664 (33 cl) 26F
Tourtel, non alcoolisée / alkoholfrei (25 cl) 24F

COFFEE SPECIALTIES
SPÉCIALITÉS DE CAFÉ · KAFFEE NACH ART DES HAUSES

MOUNT WHITNEY 40F
HOT COFFEE WITH BRANDY AND DARK CREME
DE CACAO, TOPPED WITH WHIPPED CREAM
Café chaud avec du brandy et de la crème
de cacao, coiffé de chantilly
Heißer Kaffee mit Brandy und
Kakaolikör und Sahnehäubchen

Espresso 12F   Cappuccino 15F

DIGESTIFS

Bas Armagnac, Duc de Lauzanc 40F   Calvados Hors d'Age 50F
Remy Martin V.S.O.P. 50F   Remy Martin X.O. 70F
Hennessy V.S.O.P. 50F   Germain-Robin California Brandy 100F

LIQUEURS · LIKÖRE

Benedictine 50F   Amaretto 50F

EAU-DE-VIE · BRANNTWEIN

MASSENEZ
Mirabelle 50F   Framboise 50F
Poire William 50F

Net Prices / Prix Nets / Nettopreise
Alcools 4 et 6 cl, Whiskies 4 cl, Fins 18 cl

restaurant
Sol y Sombre *(Hotel Principe Felipe)*

location
Murcia, Spain

design firm
David Carter Design

designer/illustrator
Lori Wilson

copywriter
Hotel Principe Felipe

year produced
1993

paper stock
Champion Kromecote

typeface
Futura

printing technique
Offset Lithography

number of color inks
Three PMS

number produced
500

CONCEPT

Sol y Sombre's menu incorporates the use
of dark and light design elements that play
off the "light and shadow" game.
Removable inserts are printed in both
Spanish and English.

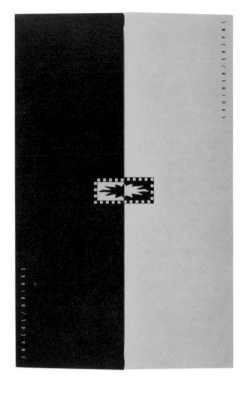

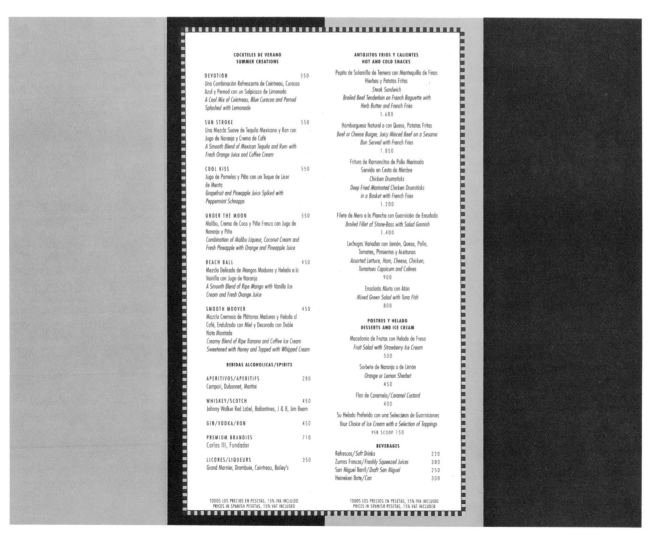

COCKTELES DE VERANO
SUMMER CREATIONS

DEVOTION   550
Una Combinación Refrescante de Cointreau, Curacao
Azul y Pernod con un Salpicazo de Limonada
*A Cool Mix of Cointreau, Blue Curacao and Pernod
Splashed with Lemonade*

SUN STROKE   550
Una Mezcla Suave de Tequila Mexicana y Ron con
Jugo de Naranja y Crema de Café
*A Smooth Blend of Mexican Tequila and Rum with
Fresh Orange Juice and Coffee Cream*

COOL KISS   550
Jugo de Pomelos y Piña con un Toque de Licor
de Menta
*Grapefruit and Pineapple Juice Spiked with
Peppermint Schnapps*

UNDER THE MOON   550
Malibu, Crema de Coco y Piña Fresca con Jugo de
Naranja y Piña
*Combination of Malibu Liqueur, Coconut Cream and
Fresh Pineapple with Orange and Pineapple Juice*

BEACH BALL   450
Mezcla Delicada de Mangos Maduros y Helado a la
Vainilla con Jugo de Naranja
*A Smooth Blend of Ripe Mango with Vanilla Ice
Cream and Fresh Orange Juice*

SMOOTH MOOVER   450
Mezcla Cremosa de Plátanos Maduros y Helado al
Café, Endulzado con Miel y Decorado con Doble
Nata Montada
*Creamy Blend of Ripe Banana and Coffee Ice Cream
Sweetened with Honey and Topped with Whipped Cream*

BEBIDAS ALCOHOLICAS/SPIRITS

APERITIVOS/APERITIFS   280
Campari, Dubonnet, Martini

WHISKEY/SCOTCH   450
Johnny Walker Red Label, Ballantines, J & B, Jim Beam

GIN/VODKA/RON   450

PREMIUM BRANDIES   710
Carlos III, Fundador

LICORES/LIQUEURS   350
Grand Marnier, Drambuie, Cointreau, Bailey's

ANTOJITOS FRIOS Y CALIENTES
HOT AND COLD SNACKS

Pepito de Solomillo de Ternera con Mantequilla de Finas
Hierbas y Patatas Fritas
*Steak Sandwich
Broiled Beef Tenderloin on French Baguette with
Herb Butter and French Fries*
1.600

Hamburguesa Natural o con Queso, Patatas Fritas
*Beef or Cheese Burger, Juicy Minced Beef on a Sesame
Bun Served with French Fries*
1.050

Fritura de Ramoncitos de Pollo Marinado
Servido en Cesta de Mimbre
*Chicken Drumsticks
Deep Fried Marinated Chicken Drumsticks
in a Basket with French Fries*
1.200

Filete de Mero a la Plancha con Guarnición de Ensalada
Broiled Fillet of Stone-Bass with Salad Garnish
1.400

Lechugas Variadas con Jamón, Queso, Pollo,
Tomates, Pimientos y Aceitunas
*Assorted Lettuce, Ham, Cheese, Chicken,
Tomatoes Capsicum and Colines*
900

Ensalada Mixta con Atún
Mixed Green Salad with Tuna Fish
800

POSTRES Y HELADO
DESSERTS AND ICE CREAM

Macedonia de Frutas con Helado de Fresa
Fruit Salad with Strawberry Ice Cream
500

Sorbete de Naranja o de Limón
Orange or Lemon Sherbet
450

Flan de Caramelo/Caramel Custard
400

Su Helado Preferido con una Selección de Guarniciones
Your Choice of Ice Cream with a Selection of Toppings
PER SCOOP 150

BEVERAGES

Refrescos/Soft Drinks	220
Zumos Frescos/Freshly Squeezed Juices	380
San Miguel Barril/Draft San Miguel	250
Heineken Bote/Can	300

TODOS LOS PRECIOS EN PESETAS, 15% IVA INCLUIDO
PRICES IN SPANISH PESETAS, 15% VAT INCLUDED

TODOS LOS PRECIOS EN PESETAS, 15% IVA INCLUIDO
PRICES IN SPANISH PESETAS, 15% VAT INCLUDED

restaurant
Fisherman's Wharf *(Newport Bay Club)*

location
Euro Disney, Paris, France

design firm
David Carter Design

designer/illustrator
Lori Wilson

year produced
1992

CONCEPT

Fisherman's Wharf is a small nautically themed bar at Euro Disney's Newport Bay Club. Striping, anchors, and sailing maps are just a few of the details found in the interiors. These elements were incorporated into the design of the menu to create a harmonizing look with the interior design and further established the thematic approach.

paper stock
Simpson Starwhite Vicksburg

typeface
Berkeley

printing technique
Offset Lithography

number of color inks
Four-color Process, Two PMS

number produced
250

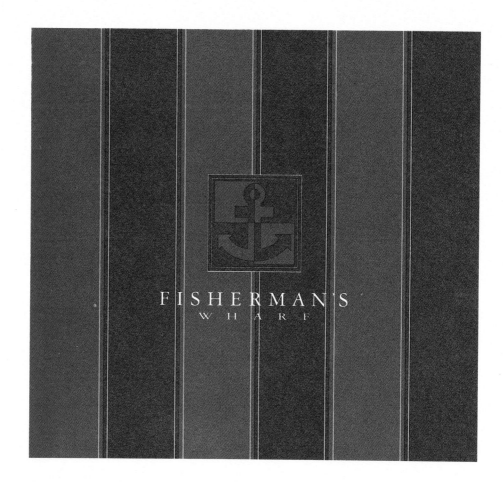

Specialty Drinks · Boissons Maison · Getränke Des Hauses

BERRY FREEZE 28 F
Jus de pamplemousse et purée de fraises frappés
Grapefruitsaft mit wild schaumig geschlagenem Erdbeerpüree

SEA SCAPES 22 F
Mélange stimulant de jus d'airelle et d'orange allégé par un doigt de Sprite
Der gesunde Geschmack von Preiselbeer- und Apfelsinensaft, mit einem Schuß Sprite

SEA BREEZE 40 F
Le drink des brachés - du vodka avec le jus d'airelle garni d'un quart de citron vert
Das Getränk der Eingeweihten - Wodka und Preiselbeersaft mit einer Scheibe Limone garniert

SCHOONER 40 F
Le favouri des corsaires - mélange de rhum blanc et du Coca garni de citron
Lieblingsgetränk der Korsaren - heller Rum und Coca-Cola mit einer Scheibe Zitrone

AMERICAN KIR 40 F
Whidbey's liqueur de "Loganberry" et vin pétillant, Domaine Ste. Michelle
Likör aus Loganbeeren mit Sekt, Domaine Ste. Michelle

YACHTSMAN'S COCKTAIL 50 F
Le cocktail des yacht-club, rien que du gin et du vermouth sec, avec un petit oignon perlé blotti au fond du verre
Der Cocktail des Yachtsclubs, einfach Gin und trockener Wermut, am Boden des Glases eine Perlzwiebel

Wine by the Glass · Vin au Verre · Weine pro Glas

Domaine Ste. Michelle, vin pétillant, Washington State, N.V. 25 F

Taittinger Brut "La Française", N.V. 25 F

Fetzer, Sundial, Chardonnay, Mendocino, 1990 25 F

Mâcon Village, Joseph Drouhin, 1990 25 F

Columbia Crest, Cabernet Sauvignon, Washington State, 1988 25 F

Mouton Cadet Rouge, 1988/89 25 F

Beer · Bière · Bier

BUD (35.5 CL) 24 F
Américaine · Amerikanisch

SAMUEL ADAMS (35.5 CL) 26 F
Américaine · Amerikanisch

KRONENBOURG 1664 (33 CL) 26 F
Française · Französisch

TOURTEL, NON-ALCOHOLIC (25 CL) 24 F
Française · Französisch

Net Prices / Prix Nets / Nettopreise

FW1 3-92 1200   Vin: 18 cl

© DISNEY

restaurant
Carnival Cruise Lines

location
Miami, Florida

design firm
Associates Design

designers
Roberta Serafini
Donna Sommerville
Jill Arena

year produced
1992-93

CONCEPT

Carnival's updated cocktail list generates excitement with its vivid colors and easy-to-read brochure format. The vibrant color design is represented on both sides of the menu, allowing it to stand alone as a table tent. This cocktail list is used aboard all of the ships in Carnival's fleet.

paper stock
100# Warren LOE Dull Enamel White

typeface
Triumvirate

printing technique
Offset Lithography

number of color inks
Four-color Process
Gloss and Dull Spot Varnish

design budget
$40,000

WINES

1	KORBEL, Brut, 187 ml, Split-Cork	4.95
2	KORBEL, Rose, 187 ml, Split-Cork	4.95
205	KORBEL, Brut	19.00
207	MOET & CHANDON, White Star	55.00
208	MOET & CHANDON, White Star, Half	32.00
201	ASTI SPUMANTE	14.00
211	CHABLIS, Callahan Hill	12.00
216	CHARDONNAY, Fetzer "Sundial"	19.00
217	CHARDONNAY, Fetzer "Sundial" (Half)	11.00
219	CHARDONNAY, Murphy-Goode, 1990	28.00
237	LIEBFRAUMILCH, St. Jacob	12.00
240	LIEBFRAUMILCH, Blue Nun (Half)	8.00
244	CHARDONNAY, Black Opal, 1990/91	20.00
257	WHITE ZINFANDEL, Bel Arbors, California (Half)	8.00
258	WHITE ZINFANDEL, Beringer, California	16.00
263	CABERNET SAUVIGNON, Domane Michel, 1987	20.00
285	CHIANTI, Nozzolini (Straw Bottle)	15.00
296	LATE HARVEST SEMILLON, Penfolds, Australia, 1987	14.00

WINES
Main Bar Only

4	CHARDONNAY, Fetzer "Sundial"	4.00
5	CHARDONNAY, Murphy-Goode, 1990	5.50
6	SAUVIGNON BLANC, Lanche	3.75
7	WHITE ZINFANDEL, Beringer, California	3.25
8	CABERNET SAUVIGNON, Domane Michel, 1987	4.25
9	CHATEAUNEUF-DU-PAPE, Chateau de Vaudieu, 1989	6.00

HOUSE SELECTIONS
2.95

10	HOUSE WHITE
11	HOUSE RED
12	HOUSE ROSE
13	WHITE ZINFANDEL
14	HOUSE CHAMPAGNE
15	CHAMPAGNE COCKTAIL
16	CHAMPAGNE MIMOSA

For your dining convenience you may order wines for dinner daily at the Main Bar Only

BEVERAGE & SERVICE

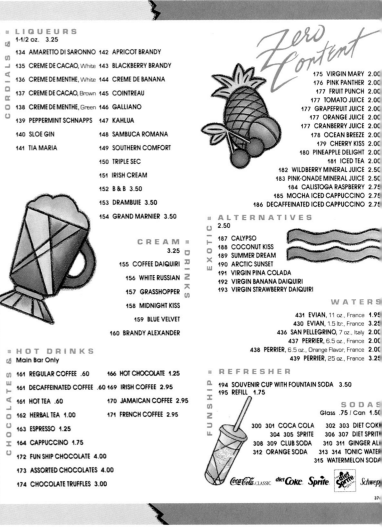

LIQUEURS
1-1/2 oz. 3.25

134	AMARETTO DI SARONNO	142 APRICOT BRANDY
135	CREME DE CACAO, White	143 BLACKBERRY BRANDY
136	CREME DE MENTHE, White	144 CREME DE BANANA
137	CREME DE CACAO, Brown	145 COINTREAU
138	CREME DE MENTHE, Green	146 GALLIANO
139	PEPPERMINT SCHNAPPS	147 KAHLUA
140	SLOE GIN	148 SAMBUCA ROMANA
141	TIA MARIA	149 SOUTHERN COMFORT
		150 TRIPLE SEC
		151 IRISH CREAM
		152 B & B 3.50
		153 DRAMBUIE 3.50
		154 GRAND MARNIER 3.50

CREAM
3.25

155	COFFEE DAIQUIRI
156	WHITE RUSSIAN
157	GRASSHOPPER
158	MIDNIGHT KISS
159	BLUE VELVET
160	BRANDY ALEXANDER

HOT DRINKS
Main Bar Only

161	REGULAR COFFEE .60	166 HOT CHOCOLATE 1.25
161	DECAFFEINATED COFFEE .60	169 IRISH COFFEE 2.95
161	HOT TEA .60	170 JAMAICAN COFFEE 2.95
162	HERBAL TEA 1.00	171 FRENCH COFFEE 2.95
163	ESPRESSO 1.25	
164	CAPPUCCINO 1.75	
172	FUN SHIP CHOCOLATE 4.00	
173	ASSORTED CHOCOLATES 4.00	
174	CHOCOLATE TRUFFLES 3.00	

Carnival

Zero Content

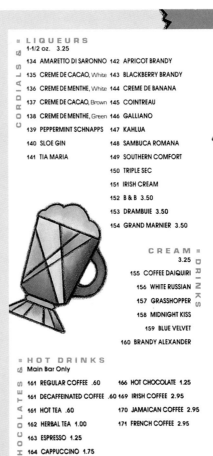

175	VIRGIN MARY	2.00
176	PINK PANTHER	2.00
177	FRUIT PUNCH	2.00
177	TOMATO JUICE	2.00
177	GRAPEFRUIT JUICE	2.00
177	ORANGE JUICE	2.00
177	CRANBERRY JUICE	2.00
178	OCEAN BREEZE	2.00
179	CHERRY KISS	2.00
180	PINEAPPLE DELIGHT	2.00
181	ICED TEA	2.00
182	WILDBERRY MINERAL JUICE	2.50
183	PINK-ONADE MINERAL JUICE	2.50
184	CALISTOGA RASPBERRY	2.75
185	MOCHA ICED CAPPUCCINO	2.75
186	DECAFFEINATED ICED CAPPUCCINO	2.75

EXOTIC ALTERNATIVES
2.50

187	CALYPSO
188	COCONUT KISS
189	SUMMER DREAM
190	ARCTIC SUNSET
191	VIRGIN PINA COLADA
192	VIRGIN BANANA DAIQUIRI
193	VIRGIN STRAWBERRY DAIQUIRI

WATERS

431	EVIAN, 11 oz., France	1.95
430	EVIAN, 1.5 ltr., France	3.25
436	SAN PELLEGRINO, 7 oz., Italy	2.00
437	PERRIER, 6.5 oz., France	2.00
438	PERRIER, 6.5 oz., Orange Flavor, France	2.00
439	PERRIER, 25 oz., France	3.25

REFRESHER

194	SOUVENIR CUP WITH FOUNTAIN SODA 3.50
195	REFILL 1.75

SODAS
Glass .75 / Can 1.50

300 301	COCA COLA	302 303	DIET COKE
304 305	SPRITE	306 307	DIET SPRITE
308 309	CLUB SODA	310 311	GINGER ALE
312	ORANGE SODA	313 314	TONIC WATER
		315	WATERMELON SODA

Coca-Cola CLASSIC   diet Coke   Sprite   diet Sprite   Schweppes

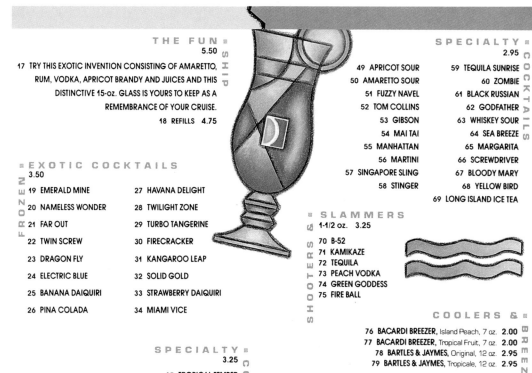

THE FUN SHIP
5.50

17 TRY THIS EXOTIC INVENTION CONSISTING OF AMARETTO, RUM, VODKA, APRICOT BRANDY AND JUICES AND THIS DISTINCTIVE 15-oz. GLASS IS YOURS TO KEEP AS A REMEMBRANCE OF YOUR CRUISE.

18 REFILLS 4.75

FROZEN EXOTIC COCKTAILS
3.50

19 EMERALD MINE	27 HAVANA DELIGHT
20 NAMELESS WONDER	28 TWILIGHT ZONE
21 FAR OUT	29 TURBO TANGERINE
22 TWIN SCREW	30 FIRECRACKER
23 DRAGON FLY	31 KANGAROO LEAP
24 ELECTRIC BLUE	32 SOLID GOLD
25 BANANA DAIQUIRI	33 STRAWBERRY DAIQUIRI
26 PINA COLADA	34 MIAMI VICE

SPECIALTY COCKTAILS
3.25

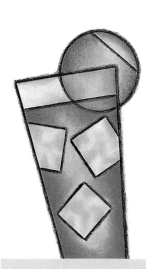

35 TROPICAL TEMPER
36 BERMUDA TRIANGLE
37 SMOOTH SAILING
38 ISLAND DELIGHT
39 ULTIMATE SUNTAN
40 TYPHOON TWISTER
41 TROPIC STAR
42 GREEN DRAGON
43 TROPICAL ITCH
44 PEACH PLEASURE
45 OCEAN DEEP
46 MANGO MANIAC
47 PEACH BREEZE
48 BURNING BULL

SPECIALTY COCKTAILS
2.95

49 APRICOT SOUR	59 TEQUILA SUNRISE
50 AMARETTO SOUR	60 ZOMBIE
51 FUZZY NAVEL	61 BLACK RUSSIAN
52 TOM COLLINS	62 GODFATHER
53 GIBSON	63 WHISKEY SOUR
54 MAI TAI	64 SEA BREEZE
55 MANHATTAN	65 MARGARITA
56 MARTINI	66 SCREWDRIVER
57 SINGAPORE SLING	67 BLOODY MARY
58 STINGER	68 YELLOW BIRD
	69 LONG ISLAND ICE TEA

SHOOTERS & SLAMMERS
1-1/2 oz. 3.25

70 B-52
71 KAMIKAZE
72 TEQUILA
73 PEACH VODKA
74 GREEN GODDESS
75 FIRE BALL

COOLERS & BREEZERS

76 BACARDI BREEZER, Island Peach, 7 oz. **2.00**
77 BACARDI BREEZER, Tropical Fruit, 7 oz. **2.00**
78 BARTLES & JAYMES, Original, 12 oz. **2.95**
79 BARTLES & JAYMES, Tropicale, 12 oz. **2.95**

DOMESTIC BEERS
2.50

80 COORS
81 BUDWEISER
82 MILLER LITE
83 COORS LIGHT
84 MILLER GENUINE DRAFT

IMPORTED BEERS

85 RED STRIPE 2.95
86 HEINEKEN 2.95
87 AMSTEL LIGHT 2.95
88 KRONENBOURG 2.95
89 LA BATTS BLUE 2.95
90 GROLSCH, 16 oz. 4.50

NON-ALCOHOLIC BEERS

91 SHARP'S 2.50
92 BUCKLER'S, Heineken 2.95
93 GROLSCH 2.95

SERVICE

Carnival.

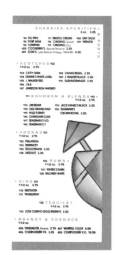

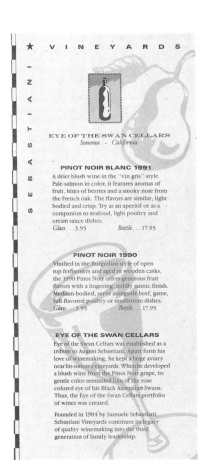

restaurant
Ramada Renaissance Hotels and Resorts
(Spring Wine Promotion)

location
nationwide

design firm
Associates Design

art director
Charles Polonsky

designers
Donna Sommerville
Jill Arena

illustrator
Donna Sommerville

year produced
1993

CONCEPT

Wine produced in the United States was the subject of Renaissance Hotels and Resorts Spring Wine Promotion. These informational half-fold pieces were both used as table menus in Renaissance Hotels throughout the country, and as as direct-mail pieces to attract customers to hotel outlets supporting the promotion. The "Made in the USA" inscription frames the Statue of Liberty design, conveying an all-American theme.

paper stock
French Speckletone

typefaces
Galliard, Engravers Roman, Univers

printing technique
Offset Lithography

number of color inks
Four-color Process

number produced
20,000

restaurant
Rip Tide Lounge

location
**Walt Disney World,
Lake Buena Vista, Florida**

design firm
David Carter Design

designer/illustrator
Kevin Prejean

year produced
1990

CONCEPT

The menu is designed literally to reflect
the rolling waves of a riptide. Each page
graduates in size, creating the look of a
cresting wave.

SPECIAL VISUAL EFFECTS

Bright, fun colors were used to complement the room's interior design.

paper stock
Starwhite Vicksburg

typefaces
Futura Condensed, Lithos

printing technique
Die-cut, Solid Ink Coverage

number of color inks
Five

number produced
500

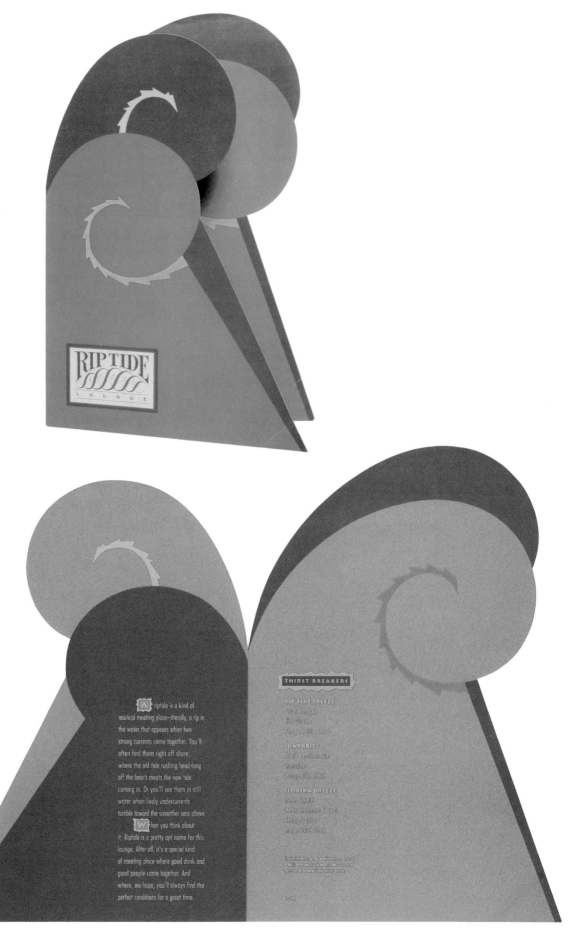

restaurant
Nantucket Pool Bar *(Newport Bay Club)*

location
Euro Disney, Paris, France

design firm
David Carter Design

designer/illustrator
Lori Wilson

year produced
1992

CONCEPT

With its vibrant colors, geometrical design, and anchor, this menu is designed to mimic nautical flags.

SPECIAL VISUAL EFFECTS

Hardwood block was custom fabricated.

paper stock
Champion Kromecote

typeface
Lubalin

printing technique
Offset Lithography

number of color inks
Five PMS

number produced
500

restaurant
Tusk Bar *(The Palace of the Lost City)*

location
Sandown, South Africa

design firm
David Carter Design

art director/designer
Randall Hill

illustrator
Lori Wilson

year produced
1992

CONCEPT

The Tusk Bar's menu reflects the sophisticated African atmosphere of The Palace of the Lost City hotel.

SPECIAL VISUAL EFFECTS

The graphic look was achieved by illustrating cave paintings on fine art paper.

TRENDS FOR THE '90s

"...laser printed menus are becoming more and more common. This poses new challenges for graphic designers and their ability to create new ideas within the constraints of computer technology. We feel this has played an important role in the introduction of unique binding systems (such as twigs, screws and even bones)..."

paper stock
Premium Coated #1 Recycled

typeface
Lithos

printing technique
Offset Lithography

number of color inks
Four PMS Match Inks

number produced
10,000

KLEIN & WILSON PHOTOGRAPHY

restaurant
La Tour Bar *(Chicago Park Hyatt)*

location
Chicago, Illinois

design firm
Associates Design

art director
Charles Polonsky

designers
Jill Arena
Donna Sommerville

illustrator
Jill Arena

CONCEPT

The French expressionistic painting pictured on the cover of La Tour Bar Wine Tasting Menu is derived from a wall mural exhibited in the restaurant. Fitting with the French flair of the menu, handmade paper is integrated around the illustration.

paper stock
Gilbert Oxford

typeface
Garamond

printing technique
Offset Lithography

number of color inks
Four-color Process
One PMS Color Insert

number produced
1,000

*W*e have created our wine and food flights to allow you to distinguish specific characteristics and descriptors in wine evaluation.

The individual "flights" are set up to assist you in discerning the nuances of these characteristics. Experiment and enjoy!

RED WINES

Bin#	Vintage	MERLOT	2 oz. Taste	5 oz. Glass	Bottle
HSE	1989	Christian Mouiex, *Bordeaux*	1.80	4.55	25.00
451	1990	Hogue Cellars, *Washington*	2.00	5.00	25.00
459	1989	Matanzas Creek, *Sonoma*	3.75	9.35	45.00
173	1988	Chateau Soutard, *St. Emilion*	3.75	9.35	45.00
		PINOT NOIR			
HSE	N.V.	Grateful Red, *Red Hawk Winery, Oregon*	2.00	5.00	25.00
239	1987	Santenay, *F. Chauvenet*	2.00	5.00	25.00
441	1989	Mondavi Reserve, *Napa*	3.50	8.75	42.00
207	1984	Clos de la Roche, *Domaine Ponsot*	6.25	15.60	75.00
221	1988	Pernand-Vergelesses, *Ile des Vergelesses, Domaine Chandon Briailles*	3.50	8.75	42.00
		SANGIOVESE			
479	1987	Broccato, *Diavole, Tuscany*	2.65	6.50	32.00
		ZINFANDEL			
447	1988	Deloach, *Sonoma*	1.65	4.00	18.00
HSE	1991	White Zinfandel, *Amador Foothills Winery*	1.65	4.00	18.00

restaurant
Harris Ranch

location
Coalinga, California

design firm
Associates Design

art director
Charles Polonsky

designer
Beth Finn

photographer/illustrator
Beth Finn

year produced
1993

CONCEPT

Harris Ranch's menus capture the bar's Western/Southwestern flair and reflect the restaurant's elegant, cozy and rustic interior of white-washed wood, cow hides and rusted iron.

The main menu, a hand-colored duotone, features a background adorned with handmade paper, while the beverage menu is a duotone displaying a leather-like textured border and wood background.

paper stock
French Speckletone

typefaces
Barcelona, Univers

printing technique
Offset Lithography

number of color inks
Four *(cover)*
Two *(inside)*
One PMS

number produced
500 each

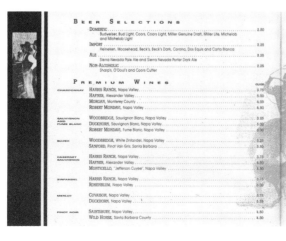

AFTERWORD

Imagination is what restaurants are all about.

How do you create "ambiance" in a restaurant? You see to it that your overall "concept" permeates every part of your operation, from the server's greeting to the folder in which the bill is presented. In other words, all parts must be subordinated to the total effect. And those words come remarkably close to S.T. Coleridge's famous description of how the imagination works.

Each year the National Restaurant Association's Great Menu Contest honors those menus that set standards in design and marketing for the foodservice industry. And each year our judges quite rightly lament their inability to experience the restaurants represented by the menus they must judge. They want to see how the menu functions within the overall design of the operation. The mark of a great menu is that it conveys the spirit of the restaurant and acts cohesively with other decor elements to create an ambiance that sets the operation apart from all others.

Many of the winners of the Great Menu Contest have appeared on the pages of this book, designated by a blue ribbon. Our judges will be delighted to see them placed back in their appropriate contexts. People often say that the menu is the greatest promotional tool a restaurateur has, but in fact, it is just one part of a total promotional system that encompasses every sensuous object connected with the establishment. As the examples presented here suggest, when all the parts speak in rhymes that reinforce each other, the patron gets the message.

Jeffrey R. Prince
National Restaurant Association

GREAT MENU CONTEST

The National Restaurant Association's annual Great Menu Contest offers foodservice operators a chance to earn recognition from their peers on the basis of their menus.

Menus are judged by a panel of food writers, editors and designers in nine categories: restaurant average check under $8 per person; restaurant average check $8-$15 per person; restaurant average check over $15 per person; institutional foodservice; banquet/catering; specialty; most imaginative; best design; and greatest merchandising power.

The judges score the entries on imagination, design and merchandising power. The winners of the Great Menu Contest receive a wooden plaque and menu stickers to display in their operations. These standard-setting menus are also displayed at the Association's Restaurant Hotel-Motel Show in Chicago and receive nationwide publicity. Many of the winners receive further exposure by their inclusion in this beautifully produced menu design book.

The Great Menu Contest is open to all foodservice operators. Designers are also welcome to enter, as long as the entry form is signed by the foodservice operator they represent. Contest entry forms are mailed in November and the deadline for entries is the end of February.

For information about the contest, contact the
National Restaurant Association, Communications Department,
1200 17th Street, N.W., Washington, D.C., 20036

or call 202-331-5900 or 1-800-424-5156.

Design Tips for
RESTAURANT & FOOD GRAPHICS

Paper Stock Selection Durable paper stocks are a common request in the restaurant industry. Consider using substrates that are pleasant to touch, that don't get sticky, but at the same time can be kept clean. As many coatings are available, designers have the option of choosing uncoated papers and treating them with lacquer or laminates to protect them.

Typography/Calligraphy Typestyle sets the tone and the attitude of the establishment. The choice of typestyle depends on the restaurant's needs and the typestyle's overall applications. Some typestyles tend to work better in smaller text style menu descriptions. A designer can assign a family of typestyles suitable for all applications in the graphic identity system. Some restaurants have even designed their own custom typefaces.

Size/Shape The most appealing aspect of restaurant graphics is that there is just about no limitation on size or shape. Consider the size of the tables and the amount of free wall space when conceptualizing the design. One interesting design solution used the shirts on the backs of the wait staff to advertise the menu offerings. Creativity can run rampant in this industry. There are not many rules to be broken. The element of surprise is what makes restaurant and food graphics so exciting.

Color Graphic design palettes which borrow from the interior and exterior architectural tones always seem to have a cohesive identity. This intermixing can go vice versa, where the interior color scheme borrows from the colors in the identity system. The most dramatic results come from the collaborative efforts of the graphic designer and interior architects.

Special Features/Printing Techniques Restaurant graphics are not limited to any particular materials. All kinds of substances can be applied in graphic identity systems, such as plastics, woods, metals–even glass. Sometimes the choice of materials is inspired from surfaces used in the decor. The important guideline here is that the materials chosen work well with the overall theme of the restaurant.

Budget/Quantity Cost is always a concern. Working smart can be most effective when planning is part of the process. Understanding the applications for the graphics can influence or detract from certain solutions. Flexibility is also a key concern, since the need to be responsive and fresh applies in restaurant and food graphics. Another consideration is that the cost to reproduce items be realistic to the quantities needed. This may dictate the complexity or simplicity of the overall graphic identity system.

Environmental Responsibility Environmental concerns can outweigh the desire for durability but the theory is that if it is durable, it will last longer and there won't be waste. If the printed items change on a frequent basis, thereby creating waste, consider using a recycled paper stock. The paper must contain post-consumer waste–just being recycled is not enough.

DIRECTORY OF DESIGN FIRMS

Aardvark Graphics
1300 Bel-Red Road, #201
Bellevue, Washington 98005
(206) 453-6010

Amalgamation House, Inc.
1218 Shackamaxon Street
Philadelphia, Pennsylvania 19125
(215) 427 1954

Associates Design
3177 Mac Arthur Boulevard
Northbrook, Illinois 60062
(708) 498-1550

Axis Design Associates, Inc.
21 Plantation Drive
Atlanta, Georgia 30324
(404) 365-0979

The Baker Agency
14850 Montfort, Suite 197
Dallas, Texas 75240
(214) 661-1186

Becker Design
225 East St. Paul Avenue
Milwaukee, Wisconsin 53202
(414) 224-4942

Belyea Design
1007 Tower Building
1809 7th Avenue
Seattle, Washington 98101
(206) 682-4895

Big Road Blue Studio
66A Elm Park Road
Finchley, London
England
(81) 349-3087

Bruce Yelaska Design
1546 Grant Avenue
San Francisco, California 94133
(415) 392-0717

Blue Suede Studio
2525 Ontario Street
Vancouver, British Columbia V5T 2X7
Canada
(604) 879-2525

Claude Prettyman Design
13402 Flint Drive
Santa Ana, California 92705
(714) 838-0081

Clifford Selbert Design, Inc.
2067 Massachusetts Avenue
Cambridge, Massachusetts 02140
(617) 497-6605

Crown Printing
8500 Brandt
Dearborn, Michigan 48126
(313) 584-6700

D.A. Design
4138 Mill Street
Putneyville, New York 14538
(315) 587-8755

David Carter Design
4112 Swiss Avenue
Dallas, Texas 75204
(214) 826-4631

Design Resource
2-1-8-904 Azabujuban
Minato-ku, Tokyo 106
Japan
03-3453-4138

Desktop by Design
1022 Oak Street
San Francisco, California 94117
(415) 863-4474

Dragon's Teeth Design
419 College Avenue
Greensburg, Pennsylvania 15601
(412) 837-5799

DRi Communications
7500 North Dreamy Draw Drive, Suite 215
Phoenix, Arizona 85020
(602) 997-7777

Rod Dyer Group
8360 Melrose Avenue
Los Angeles, California 90069
(213) 655-1800

El Torito Restaurants, Inc.
2450 White Road
Irvine, California 92714
(714) 863-8639

Erica Ando Design
339 West 19th Street
New York, New York 10011
(212) 924-0895

Weslie Evans
540 Forest Avenue
Portland, Maine 04101
(207) 892-5920

Express Foods
5858 Westheimer, #110
Houston, Texas 77057
(713) 977-1922

Falco Design, Inc.
3370 South Service Road
Burlington, Ontario L7N 3M6
Canada
(416) 681-3070

Glen Group Advertising & Marketing
Box Z
Jackson, New Hampshire 03846
(603) 383-9062

Group 425
425 Battery Street, Suite 250
San Francisco, California 94111
(415) 673-6425

Guy Parsons Visual Communications Inc.
371 Coral Sands Terrace Northeast
Calgary, Alberta T3J 3K3
Canada

Hasten Design Studios Inc.
1629 K Street, NW, Suite 950
Washington, DC 20006
(202) 293-1333

Hoffman & Angelic Design
317-1675 Martin Drive
White Rock, British Colombia V4A 6E2
Canada
(604) 535-8551

Image Group Studios
3923 Cole Avenue
Dallas, Texas 75204
(214) 552-1171

Isabella von Buol
7 Carmine Street, #18
New York, New York 10014
(212) 633-6858

The Italian Oven, Inc.
Eleven Lloyd Avenue
Latrobe, Pennsylvania 15650
(412) 537-8341

Judi Radice Hays
Post Office Box 26710
San Francisco, California 94126
(415) 673-1930

Jim Moon Designs
182 Oakdale Avenue
Mill Valley, California 94941
(415) 383-5412

John Kneapler Design
48 West 21st Street, 12th Floor
New York, New York 10010
(212) 463-9774

Kenyon Press
12616 Chardon Avenue
Hawthorne, California 90250
(310) 331-4500

The Levy Restaurants
980 North Michigan Avenue
Chicago, Illinois 60611
(312) 664-8200

Marie P. Flaherty Arts & Design
28 Jackson Street
Quincy, Massachusetts 02169
(617) 773-3653

Martelle Design
2021 San Pedro
San Antonio, Texas 78212
(210) 736-2828

McCann-Erickson (HK) Ltd.
1/F Sunning Plaza
10 Hysan Avenue
Hong Kong
HX 755627

The Menu Workshop
2815 Second Avenue, #393
Seattle, Washington 98121
(206) 443-9516

Meridian 28 Design
2021 San Pedro
San Antonio, Texas 78212
(210) 736-2828

Metro Media Arts & Communication
5814 Providence Road
Charlotte, North Carolina 28226
(714) 568-2641

Michael Mabry
212 Sutter Street
San Francisco, California 94108
(415) 982-7336

Monica Banks and Company
270 Lafayette Street, #403
New York, New York 10012
(212) 226-5657

Morris Graphics, Ltd.
10 Queen Elizabeth Blvd.
Toronto, Ontario M8Z 1L8
Canada
(416) 252-6421

Nesnadny + Schwartz
10803 Magnolia Drive
Cleveland, Ohio 44106
(216) 791-7721

On the Edge
505 30th Street, #211
Newport Beach, California 92663
(714) 723-4330

PM Design & Marketing
11 Maple Terrace, Suite 3A
Verona, New Jersey 07044
(201) 857-3211

Powell Design Office
7557 Rambler, Suite 616
Dallas, Texas 75231
(214) 891-0999

Presentations, Ltd.
120F Nancy Street
West Babylon, New York 11704
(516) 491-6368

Printing Image
Post Office Box 214
Cambridge, Wisconsin 53523
(608) 423-4811

Purple Seal Graphics
Post Office Box 3041
Carbondale, Illinois 62802
(618) 453-3489

Rachel Stephens Design
161 West Wisconsin Avenue, #4000
Milwaukee, Wisconsin 53203-2602

Reeser Advertising Associates
1325 Snell Isle Blvd. N.E.
St. Petersburg, Florida 33704
(813) 894-4884

Russell Sweet
906 Prince Street
Alexandria, Virginia 22314
(703) 684-7625

Sayles Graphic Design
308 Eighth Street
Des Moines, Iowa 50329
(515) 243-2922

Ward Schumaker
466 Green
San Francisco, California 94133
(415) 398-1069

Spangler Associates
110 Third Avenue, Suite 800
Seattle, Washington 98101
(206) 467-8888

Stafford Ream, Inc.
2501 Oaklawn
Dallas, Texas 75219
(214) 522-7080

Stahl Design
116 East 48th Street
Indianapolis, Indiana 46205
(317) 283-5000

THARP DID IT
50 University Avenue
Los Gatos, California 95030
(408) 354-6726

Tim Girvin Design
1601 Second Avenue, Fifth Floor
Seattle, Washington 98101
(206) 623-7807

True Ideas
2318 West Cullom, Second Floor
Chicago, Illinois 60618
(312) 509-0996

Visual Events
171 Jefferson Drive
Menlo Park, California 94025
(415) 326-4376

Walt Disney World Design
Post Office Box 10,000
Lake Buena Vista, Florida 32830
(407) 824-2728

INDEX

Photographers

Restaurants

ACKNOWLEDGMENTS

I extend my appreciation and gratitude to all the people who contributed their time, support, and ideas. Most importantly, I would like to acknowledge all the designers and restaurateurs who continue to create the innovative designs that made this book possible.

Special thanks to the National Restaurant Association and Jeffrey Prince for inviting me to judge the Great Menu Contest. I want to acknowledge Jennifer Batty for her efforts in managing the enormous details of the contest.

I am particularly grateful to Sue Thomas, an Academy of Art student who spent her summer internship diligently working on coordinating the many bits and pieces of this book.

Most of all, I would like to thank Mark Serchuck and Penny Sibal and the art/editorial staff at PBC International—Richard Liu, Susan Kapsis, Francine Hornberger, Garrett Schuh, Lorine Bamberg and Jennifer Mateyaschuk. Special thanks to Joanne Caggiano and photographer Naum Kazhdan.

Judi Radice Hays
San Francisco

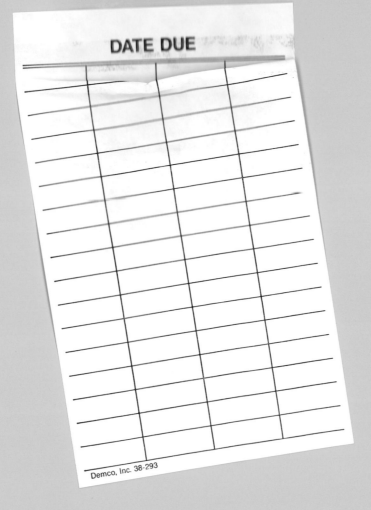

DATE DUE

Demco, Inc. 38-293